LIBYA AND NUCLEAR PROLIFERATION
Stepping back from the brink

WYN Q. BOWEN

ADELPHI PAPER 380

The International Institute for Strategic Studies

Arundel House I 13–15 Arundel Street I Temple Place I London I WC2R 3DX I UK

ADELPHI PAPER 380

First published May 2006 by **Routledge**
4 Park Square, Milton Park, Abingdon, Oxon, OX14 4RN

for **The International Institute for Strategic Studies**
Arundel House, 13–15 Arundel Street, Temple Place, London, WC2R 3DX, UK
www.iiss.org

Simultaneously published in the USA and Canada by **Routledge**
270 Madison Ave., New York, NY 10016

Routledge is an imprint of Taylor & Francis, an Informa Business

DIRECTOR-GENERAL AND CHIEF EXECUTIVE John Chipman
EDITOR Tim Huxley
MANAGER FOR EDITORIAL SERVICES Ayse Abdullah
ASSISTANT EDITOR Jessica Delaney
PRODUCTION Jesse Simon
COVER IMAGE Marwan Naamani/AFP/Getty Images
CARTOGRAPHER Steven Bernard

PRINTED AND BOUND IN GREAT BRITAIN BY Bell & Bain Ltd, Thornliebank, Glasgow

British Library Cataloguing in Publication Data
A catalogue record for this book is available from the British Library

Library of Congress Cataloguing in Publication Data

ISBN 0-415-41238-2
ISSN 0567-932X

Contents

Libya's nuclear weapons programme, 1969–2003: facilities and locations

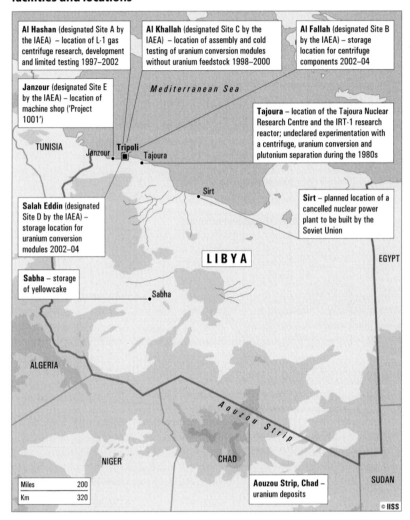

Al Hashan (designated Site A by the IAEA) – location of L-1 gas centrifuge research, development and limited testing 1997–2002

Al Khallah (designated Site C by the IAEA) – location of assembly and cold testing of uranium conversion modules without uranium feedstock 1998–2000

Al Fallah (designated Site B by the IAEA) – storage location for centrifuge components 2002–04

Janzour (designated Site E by the IAEA) – location of machine shop ('Project 1001')

Mediterranean Sea

Tajoura – location of the Tajoura Nuclear Research Centre and the IRT-1 research reactor; undeclared experimentation with a centrifuge, uranium conversion and plutonium separation during the 1980s

TUNISIA

Janzour · **Tripoli** ■ · Tajoura

Sirt ·

Sirt – planned location of a cancelled nuclear power plant to be built by the Soviet Union

Salah Eddin (designated Site D by the IAEA) – storage location for uranium conversion modules 2002–04

LIBYA

EGYPT

Sabha – storage of yellowcake

· Sabha

ALGERIA

Aouzou Strip

Miles	200
Km	320

NIGER

CHAD

Aouzou Strip, Chad – uranium deposits

SUDAN

© IISS

DISCLAIMER

The analysis, opinions and conclusions expressed or implied in this paper are those of the author and do not necessarily represent the views of the JSCSC, the Defence Academy, the UK Ministry of Defence or of any other government agency.

GLOSSARY

ANO	Abu Nidal Organisation	**OPCW**	Organisation for the Prohibition of Chemical Weapons
ADI	Arab Development Institute		
CTBT	Comprehensive Test Ban Treaty	**OTA**	Office of Technology Assessment
CWC	Chemical Weapons Convention		
HEU	Highly Enriched Uranium	**PLO**	Palestinian Liberation Organisation
IAEA	International Atomic Energy Authority		
		PSI	Proliferation Security Initiative
IDF	Israeli Defense Force	**RCC**	Revolutionary Command Council
ILP	Islamic Liberation Party		
IMM	Islamic Martyrdom Movement	**SCOPE**	Scomi Precision Engineering
ILSA	Iran–Libya Sanctions Act	**SIS**	Secret Intelligence Service
IRA	Irish Republican Army	**TNRC**	Tajoura Nuclear Research Centre
IRT-1	IRT-1 research reactor		
JIC	Joint Intelligence Committee	**UCF**	Uranium-conversion facility
LEU	Low-Enriched Uranium	UF_4	Uranium tetrafluoride
MTCR	Missile Technology Control Regime	UF_6	Uranium hexafluoride
		UO_2	Uranium dioxide
NBSR	National Board of Scientific Research	UO_3	Uranium trioxide
NOC	National Oil Corporation	U_3O_8	Uranium oxide concentrate ('yellowcake')
NPT	Nuclear Non-Proliferation Treaty	**UAE**	United Arab Emirates
NSDD	National Security Decision Directive	**UNSCOM**	UN Special Commission in Iraq
		WMD	Weapons of mass destruction

INTRODUCTION

The Libyan government announced on 19 December 2003 that it had chosen to abandon its nuclear and chemical weapons programmes, as well as to forego its long-range ballistic missile capability. The official statement announcing the decision noted that 'Libya has decided, with its own free will, to get rid of these substances, equipment and programmes and to be free from all internationally banned weapons'. The announcement took most non-proliferation practitioners and observers by surprise. It was the result of quiet negotiations involving Libya, Britain and the United States which had been the subject of intense secrecy with only a handful of officials in each government either involved in or aware of the talks. Libya would dismantle its nuclear and chemical weapons programmes completely and restrict its missile capability to systems with ranges of no greater than 300km in line with the parameters of the Missile Technology Control Regime (MTCR). A commitment was made to undertake these measures transparently, including the acceptance of international verification by the International Atomic Energy Agency (IAEA) and the Organisation for the Prohibition of Chemical Weapons (OPCW) in the nuclear and chemical fields respectively.[1]

The regime of Colonel Muammar Gadhafi had long been suspected of possessing chemical and, potentially, biological weapons capabilities. Its desire to acquire nuclear weapons was also well documented, despite Libya's status as a non-nuclear-weapon state under the Nuclear Non-Proliferation Treaty (NPT). Until Libya's decision to forego weapons of mass destruction (WMD), publicly available assessments generally concurred that – in the absence of significant and sustained injections of foreign technology and assistance – the country's technical and scientific capabilities were too under-developed to allow the indigenous development and production of nuclear weapons. However, since December 2003 it has emerged, as a result of investigations by America, Britain and the IAEA, that Libya was further advanced in the nuclear realm than previously thought.

It appears that Gadhafi's regime began seeking to acquire nuclear weapons shortly after seizing power from King Idris I in 1969. In an initial effort to procure such a capability directly 'off the shelf', the regime approached the People's Republic of China during the period 1969–71, although Beijing declined these advances.[2] China may not have been the only country contacted with this request for a weapon capability: Libya reportedly approached France in 1976,[3] India in 1978[4] and the Soviet Union in the late 1970s.[5] Moreover, Libya may also have sought to acquire a weapon via the black market.[6] Ultimately, these efforts to acquire nuclear weapons came to nothing, thus increasing the importance of finding a source for the requisite technology, materials and components to manufacture nuclear weapons domestically.

From the 1970s to late 2003, Gadhafi's regime sought to acquire key elements of the nuclear-fuel cycle from abroad, notably uranium-enrichment capabilities. Ultimately, during the second half of the 1990s, Libya became a key beneficiary of the illicit proliferation network established by Pakistani scientist Abdul Qadir Khan. The A.Q. Khan network became a pivotal 'target of opportunity' for the regime from 1997 through to 2003, with the Libyans spending millions of dollars in return for significant infusions of nuclear technology and expertise.

This paper examines Libya's pursuit of a nuclear weapons capability and the factors that in the end influenced the Gadhafi regime to forego its ambitions in this area. It begins by examining the motives underlying Libya's nuclear ambitions from the 1970s through to the 1990s. The motives, or 'drivers', are placed into context through an examination of Gadhafi's foreign and security policies, including the ideological motivations that spawned its radical approach to international relations during this period. This provides the necessary background for examining the drivers in more detail. They revolved primarily around a security imperative, specifically the regime's desire to deter external interference and intervention in Libya by states in its immediate neighbourhood and further afield.

The paper goes on to examine the proliferation pathways pursued by Libya from the early 1970s through to 2003, which are divided into three periods. The first runs from 1969 through to 1981 and encompasses Libya's initial efforts to procure the building blocks of an ostensibly 'civil' nuclear programme, ranging from uranium exploration through conversion and enrichment to the construction of research and power reactors and the reprocessing of plutonium. The second period runs from 1981 through to the mid-1990s. It encompasses Libya's active and clandestine exploration of both the plutonium- and uranium-enrichment-based routes to acquiring the fissile material required for nuclear weapons. This work occurred at the Tajoura Nuclear Research Centre (TNRC), which the Soviet Union constructed under contract to the Libyan government. The third period begins in the mid-1990s and runs to December 2003. This period witnessed the reinvigoration of Libya's nuclear efforts, particularly in the uranium-enrichment field. It was characterised most notably by the role played by the A.Q. Khan network in supporting Libya's nuclear aspirations, including the supply of gas centrifuge technology as well as weapon designs and manufacturing instructions.

The factors that contributed to the decision to forego the pursuit of nuclear weapons are then considered. The official views put forward by the Libyan, British and American governments are examined initially in order to highlight the differing emphases that they placed on various contributory factors. From the official views several factors are singled out for greater consideration, including: the effect on Libya of multilateral and unilateral American sanctions and the associated international isolation; the Gadhafi regime's change of political trajectory during the 1990s; the contribution of quiet diplomacy and negotiation involving the Libyan, British and American governments; the impact on Libyan decision-making of the war in 2003 to topple the Saddam Hussein regime in Iraq; and the impact of the intelligence-led interception of nuclear technology en route to Libya via the A.Q. Khan network.

The paper focuses on the processes by which Libya's nuclear weapons programme was dismantled in 2004 by the American and British governments, which are considered to have four main themes. First is the cooperative and non-confrontational character of the dismantlement process made possible primarily by the unilateral nature of Libya's decision. Second are the mechanisms of international verification and the Gadhafi regime's insistence on the involvement of the IAEA in particular, so that the proceedings could be verified by the international community. Third is the three-phased approach to dismantlement which was linked to the Bush administration's incremental provision of rewards to

Libya, notably the gradual removal of American restrictions and sanctions. And fourth are the ongoing issues including the priority placed on preventing a 'brain-drain' from Libya to nuclear weapons programmes in other countries.

The paper concludes by briefly addressing the question of whether there is a 'Libya Model' that may be applicable to addressing other proliferant states.

CHAPTER ONE

Nuclear 'Drivers'

The Gadhafi regime's pursuit of a nuclear weapons capability was driven primarily by a security imperative and its desire to deter external interference and intervention in Libya by states in its immediate neighbourhood and further afield. The regime identified Israel's nuclear weapons and long-range delivery capability as a significant threat. The security imperative was bolstered by the American air strikes against Libyan targets in 1986 in retaliation for Tripoli's involvement in international terrorism. The regime became concerned about similar attacks in the future and it appears that the possession of nuclear weapons, or at least creating the impression that Libya was seeking them, was seen as one way to strengthen the country's otherwise limited ability to deter external aggression. Libya's interest in nuclear weapons, and Gadhafi's frequent rhetoric supporting Arab acquisition of the atomic bomb, also reflected the regime's desire to increase its influence in the Arab world, in part by posing as its defender against Israel.[1]

Gadhafi's security and foreign policy

Following the military coup that toppled the regime of King Idris and brought Gadhafi and his associates to power in 1969, Libya's monarchy was abolished and the country declared a republic. A Revolutionary Command Council (RCC) was established to administer the country and from the outset Gadhafi and his associates ran Libya as a 'private fiefdom'.[2] This system was based on what has been described as 'a dense patrimonial system of governance' beholden to Gadhafi's 'whims and autocratic rule'.[3] Within this system all important policy decisions have been taken by Gadhafi and a small group of advisers around him, including some fellow revolutionaries, other family members and a few loyal politicians and administrators.[4] It is no surprise that Gadhafi's priority has always been the security and survival of his regime.

To help to secure and maintain domestic support, the Gadhafi regime exploited the country's oil wealth to develop a welfare state in which food, housing and clothing were guaranteed to all.[5] The regime sought to pursue domestic as well as foreign policies that were free from external influences and constraints. This goal was particularly important in terms of avoiding non-Arab interference and translated into a strong 'anti-imperialist' element in the regime's political outlook.[6] For many years a second, related foreign policy concern was to unify the Arab world. The colonial powers were perceived to have imposed artificial political boundaries on the Middle East and North Africa which served to prevent such unity.[7] In championing the cause of Arab unity, the regime advocated a non-aligned course between communism and capitalism.[8] Gadhafi's ideology was outlined most notably in 1977 as the 'Third Universal Theory' based on the four pillars of socialism, popular democracy, Arab unity and progressive Islam. This ideology shaped the external policies and activities of the Libyan state from the 1970s through to the 1990s. The theory was promoted as applicable to all countries and the regime sought to spread its influence in the region and beyond by sowing the seeds of social, economic and political change, often in violent and destabilising ways.[9] Underlying this activity, of course, was Gadhafi's overriding imperative to stay in power and the need to deter and defeat internal and external challenges that could threaten his regime's security. Ultimately, it was this priority that explains Gadhafi's quest for Arab leadership, anti-Israel policy and actions, support for international terrorism and other subversive activities. It also explains the pursuit of nuclear and chemical weapons.

Arab unity and leadership

Central to the regime's external policy was the goal of pushing Libya to the forefront of efforts to promote Arab unity. This included promoting the country as 'a defender of Islamic ideals against Western imperialism'.[10] It also involved seeking to generate the perception that Gadhafi was the true champion of Arab unity and, consequently, the only credible candidate to lead the Arab world.[11] Gadhafi was not taken particularly seriously by his Arab counterparts during the early years of his rule, and this helps to explain why he placed such an emphasis on raising the country's, and, therefore, his own, international status.

Gadhafi sought to secure a political 'union' with several Arab states during the 1970s although these initiatives ultimately came to nothing.[12] Gadhafi supported the concept of a federation of Arab states stretching from the Atlantic in the west to the Gulf in the east. One specific attempt involved Libya, Egypt and Syria establishing the Federation of Arab Republics in the early 1970s although this quickly came apart due to divergent views over 'the timing and objectives of war and diplomatic alternatives to the conflict with Israel'.[13] The failure to foster unity across the Arab world rapidly prompted the regime to support what Tripoli perceived as 'acceptable' Arab governments and to seek to bring down those deemed 'unacceptable' through subversion. Gadhafi exploited Libya's oil wealth to support subversive movements that targeted unacceptable regimes and to help to 'prop up' acceptable ones.[14] The perceived unacceptable regimes targeted through subversion at different times included Algeria, Egypt, Sudan and Tunisia. For example, Libya–Egypt relations deteriorated sharply after the uncovering in 1974 of a Libyan-backed plot against President Gamal Abdel Nasser's successor, President Anwar Sadat.[15] Moreover, in 1985 the Libyan leader called for Arabs to perform suicide attacks targeted against moderate Arab governments.[16] Not surprisingly, many Arab states turned against Gadhafi because of Libya's espousal of violent revolution. Furthermore, his support for revolutionary movements was not confined to the Arab and Islamic worlds, with assistance provided, for example, to the Irish Republican Army (IRA).[17] Libya's radical approach to external relations, both regionally and further afield, resulted in the regime's reputation as an 'unpredictable revolutionary vanguard' during the 1970s and 1980s.[18]

Anti-Israel policy and activities

An important part of selling Gadhafi's credentials in the Arab world was the hostile attitude that his regime developed towards Israel. The Jewish state was depicted as a tool of Western influence and a product of American imperialism that could only be brought down by a united Arab world. The Arab–Israeli conflict was central to the issue of Arab leadership, so Libya actively trumpeted the Palestinian cause. The regime also exploited the Arab–Israeli conflict in its competition for influence with Nasser's successors in Egypt, Presidents Sadat and Hosni Mubarak. To this end, Gadhafi sought to promote the perception that he was the only Arab leader capable of retaliating against Israel for the defeat it inflicted in the Six Day War of 1967.[19] Indeed, Libya made significant contributions to the

Arab effort in the 1973 October War by providing military equipment and financial resources.[20] The limited results of this war allowed Gadhafi to later criticise Egypt and Syria for their limited objectives. In the late 1970s, Sadat's readiness to reach a political accommodation with Israel through the Camp David accords further bolstered Gadhafi's hostility towards Egypt in his quest for Arab leadership.[21] The Gadhafi regime drew on Libya's oil wealth in an effort to isolate Israel from friends and allies by targeting small and poor states in the developing world with financial assistance.[22] Most notably, Tripoli provided radical Palestinian groups with military training and financial support to conduct acts of terrorism against Israeli and Western interests in the Middle East and Europe. The regime is reported to have provided support to Palestinian Islamic Jihad, the Popular Front for the Liberation of Palestine-General Command and the Abu Nidal Organisation (ANO).[23]

By June 1981, the Reagan administration was describing Libya as the world's 'most prominent state sponsor of and participant in international terrorism'.[24] Moreover, an Israeli report in 1986 asserted that around 7,000 terrorists were being trained in Libya by foreign experts, while sources in the US Department of Defense claimed there were 34 terrorist bases in the country.[25]

Deteriorating US relations

Tensions between the United States and Libya grew steadily during the 1970s, at first because of Gadhafi's attempts to make the Gulf of Sidra a closed bay and part of Libya's territorial waters. US–Libya relations came under increasing strain thereafter, mainly owing to Tripoli's support for revolutionary and terrorist groups. Relations soured significantly in 1979 when the Libyan authorities did nothing to prevent a mob – inspired by the Iranian revolution – from setting fire to the American embassy in Tripoli. The embassy was permanently closed in May 1980 following Libya's assassination of several Libyan dissidents in Europe.[26] The killings had been conducted under orders from Gadhafi to eliminate the 'stray dogs of the revolution'.[27] Despite the deteriorating relationship, the overall approach of the administration of President Jimmy Carter during the late 1970s has been characterised as emphasising the need to limit confrontation, to maintain economic relations and to avoid Tripoli moving closer to Moscow.[28] In terms of economic relations, several American companies had major oil concessions in Libya including Marathon Oil, Amerada Hess, ConocoPhillips and Occidental Petroleum.

During the early 1970s Libya developed strong, though primarily commercial, ties with the Soviet Union. From a Libyan perspective these were based on the regime's desire to acquire modern sophisticated weaponry to deter and defend against external aggression, and reflected its increasing isolation from the Western world because of its increasingly radical foreign policy.[29] In 1974, for example, the Soviets sealed an arms deal with Libya to provide MiG-23 and Tu-22 aircraft, T-62 main battle tanks, surface-to-air missiles and *Scud*-B surface-to-surface missiles.[30] Libya received more weaponry than it could integrate into its military, so Tripoli also began supplying arms to other governments in the developing world as a means of spreading the regime's influence. The burgeoning ties also resulted in Moscow's agreement in 1975 to provide Libya with a nuclear research reactor.[31]

As Ronald Bruce St John notes, despite the expanding relationship there was no major 'ideological affinity' between Tripoli and Moscow[32] beyond what has been described as a vague solidarity 'based on anti-colonialism, anti-imperialism, anti-Zionism, revolutionary change and "socialism"'.[33] Indeed, the Gadhafi regime openly emphasised that the country's relationship with the Soviet Union was built on commercial and not ideological foundations.[34] In a December 1979 interview, Gadhafi emphasised that while the Soviet Union was unquestionably 'a friend' there were differences between them, most notably in terms of 'religious orientation'.[35] Nevertheless, the regime attempted to move closer to Moscow in 1981 when Gadhafi sought a new arms agreement, further nuclear technology transfers, assistance in developing oilfields and a public commitment of support in the event of external aggression.[36]

US confrontation

It is no coincidence that Tripoli's overtures to Moscow coincided with the deterioration in US–Libya relations and the arrival of the Ronald Reagan administration in office in January 1981. The new administration rapidly began painting Gadhafi as a Soviet surrogate and Libya as an outlaw terrorist state. Reagan ushered in a new and highly confrontational chapter in US–Libya relations, which was characterised by a surge in terrorist attacks, many of which were linked to the Gadhafi regime, against American and Western targets.[37] In 1979 the United States designated Libya as a state sponsor of terrorism[38] and by June 1981 the US Central Intelligence Agency (CIA) was describing it as 'the most prominent state sponsor of and participant in international terrorism'.[39]

The American policy response under Reagan sought to isolate Libya on the international stage and to end its sponsorship of terrorism. According to

St John, the Reagan administration 'systematically increased' the diplomatic, economic and military pressure on Gadhafi, ranging from the closure of the Libyan People's Bureau (embassy) in Washington, advising American oil companies to begin reducing US personnel in the country, and then imposing an embargo on Libyan oil as well as 'export restrictions on American goods destined for Libya'.[40] Indeed, the United States 'imposed sanctions piece-by-piece in response to Libyan support for terrorism' which evolved into 'a comprehensive unilateral sanctions regime covering all commercial and financial transactions with Libya' under an Executive Order in 1986.[41]

The deteriorating relationship also featured military confrontation between American and Libyan forces in the Gulf of Sidra in 1981, 1983 and 1986. Moreover, a US State Department report in 1986 referred to Libya's 'meddling' in Sub-Saharan Africa, Latin America and the Caribbean, and South and Southeast Asia. A section of the report, entitled 'Character of Libyan Policy', even asserted that Libya's 'use of political, economic and military resources in support of anti-Western activities worldwide may be surpassed only by the Soviet Union, its East European allies, and possibly North Korea or Cuba'.[42]

The US–Libya relationship hit rock bottom between late December 1985 and April 1986. On 27 December 1985, 20 civilians including five Americans were killed in terrorist attacks at Rome and Vienna airports.[43] The United States asserted that Gadhafi had been involved and in January 1986 the Reagan administration adopted National Security Decision Directive (NSDD) 205, entitled *Acting Against Libyan Support for International Terrorism*. The directive stated that 'every effort will be made to seek Allied implementation of comparable economic sanctions and agreement not to replace US business and personnel'. Moreover, it was directed that 'the United States will initiate a global diplomatic and public affairs campaign to isolate Libya'.[44] In line with NSDD 205, the administration issued two executive orders in January 1986. The first declared a national emergency to deal with the unusual and extraordinary threat to the national security and foreign policy of the United States posed by the actions and policies of the government of Libya. The second implemented additional measures to block Libyan assets in the United States. Three months later, on 5 April 1986, an attack on the LaBelle nightclub in West Berlin, which was frequented by US military personnel, killed three people (including two American citizens) and injured 200 (60 of whom were American). The Reagan administration rapidly established that there was 'considerable evidence' that Libya was responsible for the explosion.[45]

The response was swift. On 15 April 1986, American aircraft, some of which were based in the United Kingdom, attacked several targets in Libya. Among others, the targets included the Azziziyah Barracks in Tripoli (the location of a command and control centre related to Libya's terrorist-related activities), the Benghazi Military Barracks (a location associated with Gadhafi's Jamahiriyah Guard) and the Murrat Side Bilal base (a training area for terrorists). According to Libyan sources the attack killed 70 people, including Gadhafi's young daughter.[46] The US government later said the attacks were aimed at 'select military and terrorist-related targets in Tripoli and Benghazi'.[47] The offensive was designed to punish the Gadhafi regime and to coerce it into ending its support for international terrorism. The inclusion of military targets may have been designed to undermine the Libyan armed forces' support for Gadhafi. Moreover, it has been suggested that a lesser objective of the American raid may have been to prompt Washington's European allies into taking more concerted action against the Libyan regime, both politically and economically, in order to avoid the United States militarily escalating the situation.[48]

Lockerbie and UN sanctions

In spite of American attempts to coerce Libya, the Gadhafi regime continued its involvement in international terrorist-related activities. In 1987, for example, a ship (the *Eksund*) loaded with arms and explosives was intercepted en route to the IRA. Most significantly, Pan Am flight 103 was blown up over Lockerbie, Scotland, on 21 December 1988 killing all 259 passengers and crew and 11 people on the ground. Two-thirds of the victims were Americans and 44 were British.[49] The subsequent investigation pointed the finger at Libya and, in late 1991, warrants were issued for the arrest of two Libyan intelligence operatives, Abd al-Baset Ali al-Megrahi and Al-Amin Khalifah Fhimah, who were accused of planting the bomb.

In January 1992, the UN Security Council adopted Resolution 731 calling on Libya to provide a full and effective response to the British and American investigation, and to a French investigation into the bombing of a UTA airliner over Africa. The resolution demanded that Libya surrender those accused, accept responsibility for the actions of its officials, pay compensation, renounce terrorism and disclose everything known about the Lockerbie attack. Libya's unsatisfactory response resulted in Resolution 748 of March 1992, which imposed sanctions on Libya. These were later strengthened by Resolution 883 of November 1993.[50] The imposition of multilateral sanctions initiated a period of change in Libya's external policies, paving the way for the resolution of the Lockerbie issue and, ultimately, the decision to forego WMD.

Nuclear 'drivers'

Libya's nuclear ambitions can only be understood against this backdrop of Gadhafi's radical and unpredictable approach to external relations during the 1970s and 1980s. It was this background that shaped the drivers of Libya's nuclear weapons programme, which primarily encompassed a security imperative.

Nuclear ambiguity

The regime's position on the nuclear issue was long notable for its ambiguity. While Gadhafi regularly claimed Libya's nuclear programme was purely peaceful in nature, he just as frequently and openly called for the acquisition of nuclear weapons in the context of an 'Arab bomb'. Although Libya signed the NPT as a non-nuclear-weapon state under the reign of King Idris in July 1968, it was not until May 1975 that the treaty was ratified by Gadhafi, primarily because Moscow had made this a condition of supplying the IRT-1 research reactor, which became operational at Tajoura in 1981.[51] The Soviets had also insisted that Libya complete a Safeguards Agreement with the IAEA and this took force in July 1980.[52] These commitments to apply nuclear technology for purely peaceful purposes were reflected in an interview with Gadhafi in December 1979:

> We have signed all agreements on the non-proliferation of nuclear weapons. Our nuclear research is conditional on international conventions. But we are as serious as the rest of the world in our desire to reduce our dependence on oil and to find alternative sources of energy including atomic sources. We are victims of the story that we want to build an atom bomb. It is not true. It is a reactionary charge that I am sorry to hear. It is against progress.[53]

Gadhafi made similar statements at various other times. In 1986, for example, he described nuclear weapons production as 'a great mistake against humanity'.[54] However, the Libyan leader was consistent in his inconsistent pronouncements on the nuclear issue. From the 1970s onwards Gadhafi also made frequent statements about the desirability of acquiring nuclear weapons. In 1976 he was reported to have remarked that 'Atomic weapons will be like traditional ones, possessed by every state according to its potential. We will have our share of this new weapon.'[55] A decade later in July 1987 Gadhafi asserted that:

> The Arabs must possess the atomic bomb to defend themselves until their numbers reach one billion, until they learn to desali-

nate seawater, and until they liberate Palestine. We undertake not to drop the atomic bomb on anyone around us, but we must possess it… If there is going to be a game using atomic bombs, then it should not be played against the Arab nation. The Arabs should have it, but we undertake not to drop it on anyone. However, if someone is going to drop one on us, or if someone is going to threaten our existence and independence even without the use of atomic weapons, then we should drop it on them. This is an essentially defensive weapon.[56]

There are many other examples of Gadhafi's contradictory statements on acquiring nuclear weapons. The ambiguity appears to have reflected under-developed strategic thinking on the part of the regime, although it did sow some uncertainty regarding Libya's intentions. It was certainly Libya's inconsistency on the nuclear front that generated significant problems for Tripoli in terms of acquiring nuclear technology and assistance for ostensibly peaceful purposes. Indeed, Libya has been generally unsuccessful in its 'legitimate' acquisition of technology and assistance from most states over the past three decades, with the main exception being the Soviet Union during the late 1970s and early 1980s.

Regime security and survival
Regime security was the key driver of Libya's nuclear aspirations as the specific value of such weapons lay in their inherent effectiveness as a deterrent. An overt declaration of a nuclear weapon capability by Libya would have made its neighbours, and external powers such as Israel and the United States, take the regime more seriously as a regional military power.[57]

Libya's vast geographical size, permeable borders and relatively small population meant that it was highly vulnerable to external intervention by hostile forces, whether from neighbouring states or from further afield. Consequently, deterring attacks that would either threaten the regime directly or indirectly challenge it by jeopardising the country's oil resources – the basis of the regime's power – took on a high priority. The regime's track-record of mischief-making in neighbouring states and its sponsorship of terrorism added to the regime's need to be able to deter external intervention.

To deter external interference, the regime attempted to create an image of Libya as a powerful regional player and actively developed its reputation for being both dangerous and unpredictable. On one level, this entailed cultivating the image of Libya as a terrorist state, including the generation of uncertainty about the regime's intentions by issuing threats and sponsoring terror attacks. On another level, Libya acquired significant quantities of sophisticated conventional weapons systems, notably from the Soviet Union but also from France, including fighter aircraft, main battle tanks and surface-to-surface missiles. These purchases were financed by Libya's significant oil wealth. However, given the country's limited manpower base, the armed forces were not large enough to assimilate all of this equipment, let alone to deter credibly potentially hostile external forces. The result appears to have been two-fold. First, the regime became a power-broker in terms of providing other states and organisations with its excess conventional weapons. Second, the regime pursued the acquisition of nuclear and chemical weapons as the only realistic option for deterring potentially hostile and militarily powerful external actors. Acquiring non-conventional weapons, or at least generating the perception that Libya was developing them, was therefore an important aspect of the regime's approach to deterrence.

Beyond the immediate North African neighbourhood, Israel was a major security concern for the Gadhafi regime and featured prominently in its nuclear calculations. From the early 1970s Israeli foreign intelligence became concerned about reports that Libya was striving to acquire nuclear weapons.[58] Given its nuclear ambitions and support for Palestinian radical groups, the Gadhafi regime presented a security issue of growing significance for Israel, so much so that it began making clear to Libya that it was far from immune to attack. As early as September 1973, Ariel Sharon, then Likud Party member of the Knesset, informed his fellow Israelis that the Israeli Defense Force (IDF) was capable of hitting 'any target in the Arab world including Libya'.[59] Israeli actions also demonstrated that it could and would act militarily if a situation were perceived to warrant a preventive or preemptive attack. Most notably this included the destruction of Iraq's Osiraq research reactor by the Israeli air force in 1981 due to concerns about Saddam Hussein's nuclear ambitions. The demonstration effect of this operation would not have been lost on Gadhafi, given that Libya's own research reactor had only recently become operational. The Osiraq operation also demonstrated that Libya's nuclear programme was, in effect, a double-edged sword – it could potentially provoke as well as deter external intervention. Four years later, in October 1985, Libya's direct vulnerability to attack was demonstrated when Israeli fighter aircraft passed undetected across Libya's coastline during an operation against the headquarters of the Palestinian Liberation Organisation (PLO) outside Tunis.[60]

It was not only Israel's conventional forces that were seen to pose a threat to the regime's security. Israel's nuclear weapons and associated long-range delivery systems were also perceived to pose a significant problem. This fact was reflected in Gadhafi's frequent references to a nuclear-armed Israel as justification to acquire a nuclear capability. For example, as a result of the Egypt–Israel peace process in the late 1970s, Libya reportedly asked Moscow for a nuclear weapon to 'create strategic parity with Israel following Egypt's departure from the Arab war coalition'.[61] In 1981, Gadhafi accused Israel of 'terrorising the Arabs with its nuclear programme',[62] and in 1985 the Libyan foreign minister, Ali Treiki, along with his Syrian and Iranian counterparts, stated that their countries would attempt to acquire nuclear weapons to counter the perceived threat from Israel's alleged nuclear arsenal.[63]

Israel continued to be a key target of Gadhafi's nuclear rhetoric over the next two decades. In an interview with Al-Jazeera in March 2002 he noted: 'We demanded the dismantling of the weapons of mass destruction that the Israelis have; we must continue to demand that. Otherwise, the Arabs will have the right to possess that weapon'.[64] Three months after Libya's decision in December 2003 to forego WMD, Gadhafi's son Saef al-Islam implied in an interview that the regime had indeed been 'developing WMD for use in the event of a conflict with Israel', but that 'progress in the Israeli–Palestinian peace process' had since made such 'planning unnecessary'.[65]

While Israel was an enduring feature of Gadhafi's nuclear rhetoric and calculations, the growing threat posed by the United States also became a significant issue, especially from the early 1980s when the Reagan administration took office. Following the American attack on Libya in April 1986, the regime became concerned about similar attacks in the future. The attack demonstrated to the regime that nuclear weapons would significantly strengthen Libya's otherwise limited capacity to deter both conventional and unconventional attacks launched by the United States or other external powers.[66] For example, referring to the 1986 attack during a televised address in April 1990, Gadhafi noted that:

> If we had possessed a deterrent – missiles that could reach New York – we would have hit it at the same moment. Consequently, we should build this force so that they and others will no longer think about an attack. Whether regarding Libya or the Arab homeland, in the coming twenty years this revolution should achieve a unified Arab nation... This should be one homeland,

the whole of it, possessing missiles and even nuclear bombs. Regarding reciprocal treatment, the world has a nuclear bomb, we should have a nuclear bomb.[67]

The American attack also prompted the Libyans in 1986 to begin concealing high-value nuclear equipment in order to avoid it being targeted. The most notable example of this at the time were the various modules of a uranium-conversion facility (UCF) that Libya had succeeded in procuring from overseas. IAEA investigations in 2004 discovered that when the modules began arriving in 1986 they were stored at locations around Tripoli.[68]

Influence and prestige

Gadhafi's frequent rhetoric calling for an 'Arab bomb' exemplified his use of the nuclear issue for political propaganda. The Libyan leader evidently played on the nuclear issue in an effort to generate greater influence within Arab politics, in particular by posing as 'a defender of the Arabs against Israel'.[69] At a press conference in November 1987 prior to an Arab summit in Amman, Gadhafi noted with regard to Israel that 'The Arabs thus have the right to manufacture nuclear weapons and to acquire the atomic bomb to defend their existence. After all, their enemy possesses this weapon, and atomic bombs are now found in the Middle East'.[70] Gadhafi made other similar statements at various times. Following the NPT Review and Extension Conference in June 1995, at which the indefinite extension of the treaty was agreed, he stated that:

> Peace will also be in danger as long as there is no balance and nuclear deterrence in the region, in that the Israelis posses[s] more than 200 nuclear warheads while the Arabs do not have a single one. The Arabs should posses[s] this weapon to defend themselves. It would be legitimate and for the sake of peace.[71]

Conclusion

In summary, Libya's nuclear weapon aspirations need to be understood against the backdrop of the Gadhafi regime's radical approach to international relations from the 1970s through to the 1990s. Security was the regime's principal nuclear driver, although Gadhafi evidently used the nuclear issue to promote his influence and position in Arab politics by seeking to promote himself as a defender of the Arabs in the face of Israeli military dominance.

While the leader's rhetoric on the nuclear issue continued to reflect these issues during the 1990s and even into the new millennium, it is now apparent that his regime did demonstrate its willingness to initiate negotiations over WMD with the United States as early as 1992 and again in the late 1990s, although nothing substantive was achieved until 2003. Nevertheless, these early attempts to open negotiations suggest that Gadhafi's nuclear calculations may have begun to change at the point that multilateral UN sanctions were imposed on Libya in 1992.

CHAPTER TWO

Proliferation Pathways

Libya's programme to acquire a nuclear weapons capability spanned just over three decades from the early 1970s to late 2003. While the programme waxed and waned in terms of the political continuity and technological momentum behind it, it was generally well financed, drawing on the country's oil wealth. By December 2003, the Gadhafi regime had succeeded in procuring from abroad most of the technical pieces of the 'nuclear-weapon jigsaw'. In this respect, the A.Q. Khan network presented itself as a major procurement opportunity from the second half of the 1990s, with Libya purchasing key equipment, materials and technology from this illicit one-stop shop. Nevertheless, by the time the regime chose to forego the pursuit of nuclear weapons, Libya had not proved capable of building on these acquisitions in any significant way. The regime was still confronted by major developmental problems in piecing together the nuclear-weapon jigsaw, owing to poor management and planning, the absence of a high-technology industrial base and a dearth of Libyan personnel with the requisite expertise and technical understanding. Moreover, while the A.Q. Khan network played a pivotal role in advancing the programme, it also put a brake on progress by not completely fulfilling Libya's requirements.

In order to examine the proliferation pathways pursued by the Gadhafi regime, the period under study can be divided into three main sections. Running from 1969 through to 1981, the first encompasses Libya's initial efforts to procure the building blocks of an ostensibly 'civil' programme, ranging from uranium exploration through conversion and enrichment to the construction of research and power reactors and the reprocessing of plutonium. The period was characterised by the general maintenance of the non-proliferation norm in relation to Libya, owing to the unwillingness of most countries to supply technology and assistance because of Gadhafi's inconsistent position on the issue of nuclear weapons. However, it was also characterised by the genesis of the Soviet–Libyan nuclear relationship including the construction of the TNRC where a Soviet-supplied research reactor became operational in 1981. The TNRC subsequently became the focal point for Libya's covert nuclear activities for the next 10 to 15 years.

The period from 1981 through to the mid-1990s encompassed Libya's active exploration of the routes to acquiring the fissile material required for nuclear weapons based on both plutonium and uranium enrichment. While the period witnessed some limited nuclear achievements by the Gadhafi regime, it was characterised primarily by significant frustration. As in the 1970s, Libya was generally unsuccessful in legitimately acquiring sensitive technology and expertise from overseas. There was also a major decrease in Soviet nuclear assistance from the mid-1980s, mainly because of Moscow's proliferation concerns. Moreover, the American attack on Tripoli in April 1986 prompted the Gadhafi regime to begin physically concealing significant elements of the programme and this served to further undermine progress.

A third period, from the mid-1990s to December 2003, witnessed the reinvigoration of Libya's nuclear efforts, particularly in the enrichment field. It was characterised most notably by the A.Q. Khan network's support for Libya's nuclear aspirations, including the supply of gas centrifuge technology as well as a weapon design and manufacturing instructions. In theory, the infusions of technology from the network should have put Libya in a position to initiate a step change in its capability to produce fissile material for nuclear weapons. In reality, however, Libya's progress was constrained by planning, technical and manpower problems.

Establishing the building blocks, 1969–81

The failure to procure nuclear weapons from China in the early 1970s demonstrated to the regime that attempts at 'off-the-shelf' procurement were unlikely to succeed. This was reflected in part by Libya's active courting of overseas nuclear technology suppliers from the early 1970s onwards. Over the decade to 1981, Libya sought assistance for all aspects of an ostensibly civilian nuclear fuel cycle ranging from uranium exploration, mining and processing, enrichment, research and power reactors (for electricity production and desalination), to plutonium reprocessing. Due to Libya's lack of home-grown scientific and technical expertise, an emphasis was also placed on securing this from overseas. During the 1970s and 1980s, Libya's Arab Development Institute (ADI) reportedly recruited scientists of various types from Iraq, Lebanon, Syria, Egypt and other Arab countries by offering large salaries, free housing and excellent working conditions.[1] The nuclear element of ADI's work was highlighted in October 1981 when the organisation hosted a conference on nuclear technology for developing countries.[2]

In terms of establishing the building blocks of an ostensibly 'civil' programme, this initial period was characterised primarily by four inter-related issues: the reluctance of many countries to sanction the supply of sensitive technology and equipment; the initiation of Soviet–Libyan nuclear relations; uranium imports from Niger; and the beginnings of a nuclear link with Pakistan.

Reluctant suppliers

The Gadhafi regime approached numerous overseas suppliers during the 1970s in its search for nuclear technology and expertise. While it received some limited assistance from non-Soviet suppliers, Libya was generally unsuccessful in acquiring significant input, mainly because of concerns about Gadhafi's inconsistent position on the nuclear issue

Nuclear cooperation agreements were pursued with several countries. In 1974, for example, an agreement was negotiated with Argentina for assistance in developing the front end of the fuel cycle, including the prospecting, mining and processing of uranium. It appears the agreement covered the provision of advice, training and equipment[3] but, according to Argentina's Investigación Aplicada,[4] the only cooperation that ultimately took place involved the training of Libyan geologists during the mid-1970s.[5]

Libya's early nuclear activities also benefited from links with Egypt. According to Shyam Bhatia, a connection with Egyptian nuclear scientists began to develop in the early 1970s and resulted in the movement across of personnel and ideas. Egyptian personnel were reportedly recruited to compensate for Libya's lack of trained manpower. Some Egyptian nuclear scientists reportedly worked in the science department of Al Fatah University in Tripoli. These scientists included Dr Eizzat Abdel Aziz, who was alleged to be Gadhafi's chief nuclear adviser at the time, and who assisted in negotiations with the French and Soviet governments 'during his six years in Libya'. Aziz subsequently directed the nuclear research centre at Inshas after returning to Egypt in 1980. Moreover, Salah Hedayat, one-time scientific adviser to Egyptian President Nasser, reportedly examined the concept of using funding from Libya to maintain the 'momentum of research and development' at Inshas and other facilities in Egypt. According to Bhatia, both Nasser and Gadhafi gave their personal support to this project but the plan was short lived following the death of the Egyptian leader in 1970. Libya–Egypt relations subsequently deteriorated after a 1974 Libyan-backed plot against Sadat was uncovered.[6]

Libya also approached, albeit unsuccessfully, both the United States and France. In 1975, the US State Department declined export licenses required by General Atomics to transfer a research reactor to Libya.[7] The contract would reportedly have entailed the transfer of a complete reactor system and some enriched uranium fuel.[8] The French government also discussed with Libya the sale of both research and power reactors. According to one report, France cancelled a 'preliminary agreement', reached in 1976, to supply a 600MWe nuclear power reactor because of strong international opposition to the deal based on proliferation concerns.[9] Libya also reportedly tried to acquire 20 calutrons to enrich uranium in 1973 from the French company Thomson-CSF, although the deal was halted by the French government.[10] Calutrons use the electromagnetic isotope separation process for enriching uranium. Libya reportedly reached an agreement with India in 1977–8 under which the latter would have provided assistance for the peaceful application of nuclear technology in exchange for cheap oil.[11] However, India limited its assistance to less sensitive areas including personnel exchanges, reactor operations, theoretical nuclear studies and the supply of laboratory isotopes for medical applications.[12] Moreover, the Indians rapidly allowed the agreement to lapse due to growing concerns about Gadhafi's intentions,[13] in particular his regime's suspected nuclear relationship with Pakistan. This was despite Libya's reported termination of its oil shipments to India in an effort to coerce New Delhi into supplying more sensitive technologies related to reprocessing.[14]

Soviet patronage

Libya's lack of success with these and other nuclear suppliers pushed it towards the Soviet Union as a source of nuclear assistance. For at least two decades from the mid-1970s, the Soviets became the most significant external influence on the progress of Libya's nuclear ambitions. Tripoli's expanding relationship with Moscow resulted in a 1975 agreement under which the Soviet Union agreed to build the TNRC, including a 10MW light-water research reactor, on condition that Libya ratified the NPT and concluded a Safeguards Agreement with the IAEA. In order to justify the provision of a research reactor and related facilities to Tripoli, Moscow applied 'stringent safeguards to Libya' but appeared 'confident enough' in its ability to influence the Gadhafi regime not to violate the Safeguards Agreement by pursuing nuclear weapons.[15]

Russia's Atomenergoexport supplied the fuel for the IRT-1 reactor on a 'turnkey' basis[16] and assisted with its construction,[17] while the Kurchatov Institute assisted in setting up and operating the reactor.[18] The first fuel shipment of 11.5kg of enriched uranium arrived in April 1981[19] and the IRT-1 became operational that August.[20] As early as 1976, American experts reportedly believed that a reactor of this size was too small for producing the quantities of plutonium required for a weapon.[21] This belief may have been based on a view that the reactor would not pose a proliferation threat because of the time it would take to produce the requisite amount of plutonium for a weapon. This could explain why the American reaction to the deal at the time has been described as 'mild'.[22] However, Moscow's ability to influence the Gadhafi regime to comply with its Safeguards Agreement was subsequently found wanting, as the reactor was later used in undeclared plutonium separation experiments during the 1980s.

In addition to Tajoura, negotiations were also conducted with the Soviet Union in the mid-1970s on the construction of a nuclear power plant at Sirt. It was agreed in 1977 that Atomenergoexport would design and construct a dual-purpose nuclear power plant for electricity generation and desalinating seawater. The plans for the facility incorporated two VVER-440 pressurised water reactors and a desalination plant capable of processing 80,000m³ of water per day.[23]

Uranium imports

Beyond its dealings with the Soviet Union, the regime sought to procure a stockpile of uranium for its nuclear programme. Despite receiving foreign assistance in the exploration field, Libya had little success in uncovering significant uranium deposits during the 1970s and early 1980s. This failure to find exploitable domestic reserves prompted the regime to seek external sources. It has even been speculated that Libya intervened in neighbouring Chad partly in the hope of exploiting potential uranium deposits located in the Aouzou Strip, which Gadhafi occupied in 1973[24] and did not withdraw from completely until 1994.[25]

Libya did succeed in acquiring significant amounts of 'yellowcake' (uranium oxide concentrate) from another neighbouring country. The IAEA confirmed in 2004 that Libya acquired 2,263 tonnes of yellowcake from two producers in Niger between 1978 and 1981. The total amount of imported uranium amounted to 1,587 tonnes stored in 6,367 containers.[26] Libya informed the IAEA that 587 tonnes of this total had been acquired prior to its Safeguards Agreement taking force in July 1980.[27] Until then, Libya had not been required to declare such imports to the IAEA. The number of containers was physically verified by the agency and the total volume of imports was also confirmed by documentation provided by the Libyans and the two uranium producers.[28] The disclosure authenticated the general accuracy of studies published during the 1980s that had drawn attention to Libya's acquisition of uranium from Niger.[29] However, there were also numerous unconfirmed reports during the 1980s that Libya had re-exported some uranium to Pakistan. Several studies claimed that significant quantities – potentially up to 450 tonnes – were transferred to Pakistan during the period from 1976 to 1982.[30] While no references were made during the IAEA investigation in 2004 to any transfer to Pakistan, it is possible that Libya may have decided to conceal such previous activity. Indeed, there has been a great deal of speculation about the nature of Libyan–Pakistani nuclear relations during the 1970s, as well as the more recent period since the mid-1990s.

The initial Pakistan connection

The nuclear relationship with Pakistan probably began during the 1973–5 period.[31] It was widely reported during the 1980s that, in return for deliveries of uranium from Niger to Pakistan's clandestine enrichment programme and financial assistance for its nuclear weapons efforts, Libya had hoped to receive technology and know-how relevant to weapons development, notably for enrichment and reprocessing.[32] In the latter field, for example, Libya reportedly sought assistance from Pakistan on 'hot cells' for extracting plutonium from irradiated uranium.[33] Indeed, Rodney W. Jones noted in 1981 that 'Libya happens to be the one country where motives, financial capabilities, and mineral geography could have smoothly converged to make the Pakistani [nuclear weapon] project feasible'.[34] Bhatia noted in 1988 that the Libyans wanted 'full access' to Pakistan's nuclear programme in return for uranium and financial assistance.[35]

The reported scale of Libya's financial assistance to the Pakistani nuclear-weapon programme during this period ranged from US$100 to US$500 million.[36] It appears that during the 1970s the Pakistan government may have initially exploited the 'Islamic' nature of its programme to generate funding and other support from countries in the Muslim world.[37] W.P.S. Sidhu has noted that the joint venture Pakistani–Libyan Holding Company, established in 1978 to promote industrial development, was regarded by some Indian observers as the channel for Libya's financial support to the Pakistani nuclear weapon programme.[38] Indeed, Libya certainly provided Pakistan with a significant amount of aid during the 1970s. In 1979 alone, Libyan loans and investments totalled US$133m.[39]

Despite the lack of clarity on the exact nature of the nuclear relationship during this period, it appears that Pakistan did provide Libya with at least some technical assistance in the form of training and personnel exchanges. In 1980, for example, 18 Libyans were reportedly trained at the Pakistan Institute of Nuclear Science and Technology, possibly at a cost of US$100m.[40] Moreover, the number of nuclear scientists from Pakistan visiting Libya steadily increased from the mid-1970s.[41] However, it does not appear that Libya received significant amounts of sensitive technology during this early period. [42]

Importantly, cooperative relations between Libya and Pakistan in the 1970s were based on the positive links between Gadhafi and Pakistan's then President, Zulfikar Ali Bhutto.[43] Gadhafi provided Bhutto with support following the 1971 Bangladesh War and Gadhafi's deputy Major Jalloud 'visited Pakistan frequently' in 1975–6.[44] However, Libyan–Pakistani relations deteriorated after Bhutto was overthrown by a military coup in July 1977. Between the coup and Bhutto's execution in April 1979 under the new regime of President Mohammed Zia-ul-Haq, this initial phase of nuclear cooperation apparently ended, although there were attempts to revive links prior to the mid-1990s.[45]

In summary, Libya had expended significant effort and resources by the early 1980s to acquire the building blocks for an ostensibly 'civil' nuclear programme. While the Gadhafi regime made some progress towards this goal by establishing a nuclear research centre and acquiring a research reactor with the assistance of the Soviet Union, it was significantly frustrated by the unwillingness of other suppliers to deal with Libya, owing to concerns about its nuclear intentions. Indeed, by 1981 Libya had become largely reliant on Moscow for the provision of nuclear technology and expertise. While the Pakistani link appeared to wane towards the end of this initial period, the connections established during the 1970s proved useful when Libya reinvigorated its nuclear programme in 1995.

Arrested development, 1981–95[46]

The launch of the TNRC and its IRT-1 reactor heralded a new phase in Libya's nuclear programme. The research centre subsequently became the focal point of the country's clandestine nuclear activities for the next

10–15 years. These activities encompassed undeclared work on uranium conversion, gas-centrifuge enrichment and plutonium separation. As in the preceding period, Libya's reliance on securing foreign technology and assistance was a key constraint: most nuclear supplier countries were unwilling to become involved with the regime owing to their proliferation concerns. A report by the US Office of Technology Assessment (OTA) in 1984 noted that Libya's nuclear aspirations had been significantly hindered 'by the weakness of its technical manpower base and lack of coherent planning and research programs'.[47]

Plutonium separation and production

It is now known that the Gadhafi regime actively explored the plutonium route to developing nuclear weapons during the 1980s, although this ultimately came to nothing. The most obvious evidence involved experiments conducted at the TNRC to separate plutonium from irradiated uranium targets. At the time, Libya concealed these experiments from the IAEA. Specifically, several dozen small uranium oxide and uranium metal targets were fabricated and subsequently irradiated in the IRT-1 research reactor during the 1984–90 period. Of these targets – each containing some 1g of uranium – 38 were dissolved and radioisotopes extracted using ion exchange or solvent extraction methods in hot cells at the radiochemical laboratory adjacent to the reactor. Very small amounts of plutonium were separated from 'at least two of the irradiated targets'.[48] In the mid-1980s Libya also sought, although unsuccessfully, to acquire additional equipment relevant to plutonium separation. For example, Argentina was approached regarding the potential transfer of a small-scale 'hot-cell' facility, but the request was turned down as a result of American pressure.[49]

While Libya evidently made some progress in terms of developing the expertise required for separation, it failed conclusively in its efforts to acquire the wherewithal to produce the amounts of plutonium required for a weapon. Although spent fuel from the IRT-1 was obviously one potential source of plutonium, the reactor's limited size meant that, while pivotal to the process of developing separation expertise, it was too small to produce the necessary quantities of plutonium. Another potential source could have been the nuclear power plant that the Soviet Union had agreed to build for Libya at Sirt. In terms of proliferation potential, one assessment in 1980 concluded that a 440MWe pressurised water reactor of the type that Libya was set to receive from the Soviets would produce around 70kg of plutonium annually.[50]

However, the deal never proceeded beyond the feasibility and design development stage. While Libya successfully concluded a technical cooperation project with the IAEA in December 1985, under which a group of experts reviewed the site for the nuclear power plant,[51] a separate project with the agency approved in 1984 – to support Libya's nuclear power development programme – was cancelled just six months later in June 1986, probably as a result of the Soviet power reactor deal expiring at around the same time.[52]

The Soviet deal appears to have expired primarily as a result of proliferation concerns and was probably influenced by the 'new thinking' in Soviet Premier Mikhail Gorbachev's foreign policy, which had begun to take hold at that time. There were also reports that Moscow may have been concerned about Libya's ability to pay the estimated US$4 billion price tag over the projected 15–18 year timeframe.[53] Contending explanations have also been put forward, such as that Libya was dissatisfied with Soviet technology, it was concerned about the safety of Soviet-supplied reactors, and that Tripoli wanted to modify the VVER reactors to improve their safety standard for the greater seismic risks on the northern coastline of Libya.[54] It is unclear to what extent the Chernobyl nuclear accident in April 1986 may have prompted concerns about the safety of Soviet reactors.

Libya did seek non-Soviet assistance for the Sirt project, including technical expertise from Bulgaria and Yugoslavia.[55] Discussions with Belgonucleaire in the mid-1980s reportedly covered architectural services and the supply of non-nuclear equipment for the Sirt facility as part of a proposed US$1bn contract,[56] although the Belgian government stepped in to prevent the deal due to American concerns.[57] A further report in 1984 suggested that Libya had been moving to a strategy of 'major contracts that would be put together by a consultant under Libyan leadership'.[58] Regardless of which explanation, or combination of explanations, most accurately explains the expiry of the Soviet deal, Libya's power reactor project came to a grinding halt in the second half of the 1980s, primarily because of concerns about Gadhafi's nuclear intentions.

The acquisition of a heavy-water reactor fuelled by natural uranium was another source of plutonium that Libya may have considered. While Libya did not manage to acquire a uranium conversion facility capable of producing uranium hexafluoride (UF_6) during the 1980s, it did succeed in producing uranium metal during uranium conversion experiments at the TNRC. If applied on a larger scale this scientific wherewithal could potentially have been used to prepare natural uranium metal from which fuel elements for plutonium production reactors can be made.[59]

Uranium conversion

The IAEA has determined that Libya began seeking to acquire a UCF 'no later than 1981'.[60] Libya's activities in this area encompassed experiments at the TNRC, requests to the IAEA for assistance in uranium fluoride production and fluoride chemistry, and the training of personnel in Eastern Europe. Activities also included failed attempts to acquire a UCF from at least two countries, but the successful procurement of a modular UCF from a company in 'a Far Eastern country', believed to be Japan, although the modules remained in storage until 1998.[61] While Libya did seek to acquire a capability to produce UF_6 for enrichment purposes, no such material was produced during its experiments and the modular UCF was not UF_6 capable.[62]

Libya conducted small-scale conversion experiments in an undeclared laboratory at the TNRC between 1983 and 1989. Small batches of feed material (34–39kg in all), which had been derived from imported yellowcake stored at Sabha were used. Libya informed the IAEA in 2004 that the purpose of the experiments was to acquire experience in the dissolution of yellowcake, the purification of uranium solutions and the production of uranium tetrafluoride (UF_4) and uranium metal. Indeed, the experiments resulted in the production of uranyl nitrate, uranium dioxide (UO_2) and uranium trioxide (UO_3), UF_4 and uranium metal.[63]

As part of its conversion programme, Libya had asked the IAEA in the early 1980s for assistance in uranium fluoride production, although the request was not fulfilled. In addition to seeking IAEA help, Libyan scientists benefited from working with foreign counterparts in the conversion field between 1983 and 1986 including some from a nuclear weapon state, assumed to be the Soviet Union because of its active nuclear assistance programme with Libya. Moreover, Libyan scientists studied fluorine chemistry 'in the mid-1980s in an East European country'.[64] This country may have been Yugoslavia.

Libya's conversion efforts also included negotiations with a West European company, beginning in 1981, for the construction of a pilot conversion plant at Sabha capable of processing 100 tonnes per year of yellowcake into UF_4. One of the options reportedly considered included the buildings and equipment for producing low-enriched UO_2 from low-enriched UF_6, and the buildings to house UF_4 to UF_6 conversion equipment, though not the equipment itself. Significantly, this would have meant omitting the equipment for producing the UF_6 feedstock required for the enrichment process. The company also proposed constructing a set of related laboratories based primarily at the TNRC but also possibly at Sabha.[65] The company involved was reportedly Belgonucleaire and the United States applied pressure on the Belgian government to prevent any deal because Libya's 'civil' nuclear programme did not have a logical use for the output of such a plant. The deal was abandoned in 1985–6.[66]

Libya also tried, unsuccessfully, to negotiate the procurement of a UCF from a nuclear-weapon state assumed to be the Soviet Union. The negotiations began in 1983 and were for a plant capable of producing 120 tonnes of natural UF_6 per year. However, Libya did ship 100kg of yellowcake to this country in 1985, 'in connection with the possible construction in Libya of a uranium conversion facility'. In February 1985, the country shipped back to Libya approximately 39kg of UF_6, 6kg of U_3O_8 (yellowcake), 6kg of UO_2 and 5kg of UF_4 (all masses refer to the uranium content). The uranium compounds were intended as sample materials for a conversion facility but Libya claimed in 2004 that the compounds were never used, and the IAEA subsequently verified this.[67]

While Libya failed in its efforts to procure UCFs from Belgium and the Soviet Union, it succeeded in ordering, from a company believed to be based in Japan, a modular UCF designed to Libyan specifications, and including a fluorination module. When the modules began arriving in 1986, they were delivered without assembly or operating instructions[68] or the fluorination module. The modules that were delivered remained in storage at locations near Tripoli for well over a decade and were not unpacked until the late 1990s.

Centrifuge enrichment

In addition to pursuing but not acquiring the capability to produce UF_6, Libya sponsored the development of gas centrifuges for uranium enrichment. This work took place in a side building at the TNRC between 1982 and 1992 with the assistance of a German engineer using a centrifuge design that he had brought with him.[69] Although a single centrifuge was reportedly running at one point during the project, Libya never enriched any uranium and no UF_6 was introduced. IAEA investigations in 2004 noted that stocks of centrifuge components from this early period include a 'small number of unfinished, maraging steel cylinders' with the 'same diameter as the more advanced L-2 centrifuges' provided to Libya in September 2000. However, the source of these cylinders is unknown.[70]

This work was supplemented by procurement activities during the 1980s, which further emphasised the regime's interest in centrifuges. For example, Libya reportedly bought a specialised furnace from Japan in 1985, and vacuum pumps from Europe.[71] Libya also acquired two mass spectrometers in the early 1980s, which were supplied by a 'foreign expert'.[72] Discussions may also have taken place in the early 1980s between Libya and Argentina on the supply of enrichment-related technologies, although these do not appear to have borne fruit.[73]

In summary, the period from 1981 through to the mid-1990s was characterised by Libya's systematic violation of the spirit and letter of its Safeguards Agreement obligations in its pursuit of the fissile material required to develop nuclear weapons.[74] The undeclared work conducted during the 1980s at the TNRC on plutonium separation, uranium conversion and gas centrifuges highlights the inherent difficulties of seeking to guarantee the purely civil use of nuclear materials and facilities when confronted by a determined proliferator such as the Gadhafi regime. While Tripoli achieved some limited advances in these areas, the period was primarily one of significant frustration. The general unwillingness of most potential nuclear-supplier countries to deal with the regime, because of concerns about its nuclear intentions and terrorist activities, certainly contributed to the lack of progress. The period also highlighted Libya's almost total reliance on acquiring nuclear technology and training from overseas suppliers. This reliance was clearest during the third and final period that ran from 1995 to the end of 2003.

Reinvigorating the nuclear programme, 1995–2003

The final period began in 1995 when the Gadhafi regime decided to reinvigorate its nuclear efforts by focusing specifically on enrichment. A key feature of the revived programme was the reduced role played by the TNRC. During this final phase, the centre ceased to be the physical focal point for clandestine activities, although it did continue as an intellectual focal point. Enrichment-related activities took place at dispersed sites, primarily because of a desire to conceal activities.[75]

The period was marked most notably by the contribution of the clandestine nuclear supply network established and operated by Pakistani scientist A.Q. Khan and his associates across Europe, Africa and Asia. The existence of this network helps to explain the revival of the nuclear programme from 1995 onwards. It has been described as 'one-stop shopping' for countries wanting 'to develop a gas centrifuge uranium enrichment programme, to procure weapons information, or to gain access to supplier contacts'.[76] According to Ambassador Donald Mahley, the senior US WMD representative in Libya in early 2004, without this network's support the nuclear threat posed by Libya would have been significantly constrained 'if not thwarted altogether'.[77] However, while the network undoubtedly presented a major opportunity for Libya, it was by no means the most reliable supplier of high-quality materials, equipment and components.

Target of opportunity

Following the decision to reinvigorate its nuclear programme, Libya contacted A.Q. Khan in 1997 and over the next six years purchased from his network a a significant number of centrifuges, as well as UF_6 and nuclear-weapon designs. The network also provided overseas training opportunities for Libyan personnel and facilitated the acquisition of other sensitive materials and equipment such as maraging steel, high-strength aluminium, flow-forming machines and precision lathes. The Gadhafi regime was fortunate in that it could draw on Libya's oil wealth to purchase key items and assistance: Tripoli spent between US$100m and US$500m on its renewed effort to develop nuclear weapons from the late 1990s onwards.[78]

The 1997 contact, which was initiated by Libyan intelligence, was reportedly followed by a meeting in Istanbul between two Libyan officials, A.Q. Khan himself and his associate Buhary Syed Abu Tahir, a Sri Lankan national. The Libyan officials notably included Matooq Mohammed Matooq.[79] Matooq was head of the National Board for Scientific Research (NBSR), the organisation in charge of Libya's nuclear-weapon programme.[80] It was previously known as the National Authority (or Academy) for Scientific Research, which was set up in 1981 to formulate and supervise 'national research policy', to 'fill in gaps in research not tackled by any existing research institutes and centres' in Libya, and to 'technically coordinate research' carried out therein. The NBSR was fragmented in nature and the TNRC, ADI and other organisations came under its jurisdiction.[81]

Libyan officials held further meetings with Khan and Tahir between 1998 and 2002, at least once in Dubai and once in Casablanca.[82] The diverse locations of the meetings reflected the complex and transnational nature of the network. Indeed, IAEA Director General Mohammed ElBaradei has since described the network as 'driven by fantastic cleverness'.[83] It involved nuclear specialists, middlemen and supplier companies from across three continents. Centrifuges were designed in one country, the components manufactured in another, shipments occurred via a third, with delivery on a 'turnkey' basis to a fourth, with no clarity about the end user.[84] In short, the Gadhafi regime placed orders with its Pakistani contacts, who then turned to middlemen who contacted suppliers to produce the components before shipping them to Libya.[85]

The network exploited countries with weak export controls such as Malaysia and the United Arab Emirates (UAE). Orders were placed with workshops for sensitive components, many of which were assembled from less sensitive items exported from Europe, thereby demonstrating loopholes in European export controls.[86] The workshops produced components based on a range of imported items, including speciality metals and sub-components. The finished items were then sent to Dubai in the UAE under false end-user certificates, repackaged and forwarded to Libya. According to one report, there were around half a dozen core workshops either manufacturing centrifuge components or assembling them. The workshops were chosen on the basis that the necessary materials and manufacturing equipment would be present to enable production of the requisite centrifuge components.[87]

The most well-known example of the network's operations related to Libya involved the Malaysian company Scomi Precision Engineering (SCOPE). SCOPE's role came to light after the German-flagged ship, *BBC China*, was intercepted by the Italian Coast Guard in the Mediterranean on 4 October 2003 following a request from the US government under the Proliferation Security Initiative (PSI). The boat was en route to Libya from Dubai and was diverted to Taranto in Italy,[88] where a consignment of centrifuge parts was discovered in crates labelled 'Scomi'.

A subsequent investigation by the Malaysian authorities revealed that Tahir had contacted Scomi (a chemical, oil and gas trading as well as manufacturing company) in February 2001. A two-year deal worth around US$3.5m was reached in December 2001 for the manufacture of thousands of 14 types of centrifuge components.[89] SCOPE was set up by Scomi as a subsidiary to fulfil its contracts, although it has since been cleared of knowing the components' purpose and destination.[90] Modern milling, turning and tooling machines were reportedly acquired for the workshop from France, Japan, Taiwan and the United Kingdom.[91] Moreover, the network reportedly acquired some 300 tonnes of aluminium tubes, via a Singapore-based subsidiary of a German company, for machining at SCOPE. In doing so, a grade of aluminium was reportedly selected that was not subject to international nuclear export control regulations relating to sensitive materials and hence would not generate suspicion. The tubes were sent to Libya in four shipments through a trading company in Dubai between December 2002 and August 2003.[92]

Workshops in Turkey also produced components for Libya's centrifuges, including motors and the frequency converters used to regulate their power. Sub-components for this equipment were imported from

Europe and elsewhere for assembly in Turkey. It was then shipped to Dubai with false end-user documentation, repackaged and sent on to Libya.[93] According to the Royal Malaysian Police, the transhipment via the UAE was arranged by Tahir for a Turkish engineer who had reportedly known A.Q. Khan since the 1980s.[94]

The UAE, and notably the Emirate of Dubai, was the focal point of the network's transhipping and acquisition activities on behalf of not only Libya but also Iran. The UAE was presumably targeted because it is one of the world's most important re-export centres.[95] As a result, it is very difficult for customs and intelligence organisations to keep track of all shipments, particularly when front companies are set up to exploit such opportunities. For example, it has been alleged that Tahir used a computer company in Dubai to move centrifuge components to recipients of the network.[96]

The A.Q. Khan network provided Libya with more than just centrifuge-related technology, materials and equipment. It also provided nuclear-related training opportunities, encompassing computerised machining techniques, gas handling, heat-treating materials, mass spectrometers, power systems, quality control and welding. For example, Tahir reportedly arranged for Libyan technicians to receive training in Malaysia on the handling of quality-control machines.[97] The Libyan government also reportedly admitted that some of its scientists travelled to Dubai to participate in training courses.[98] Moreover, seven or eight Libyan technicians allegedly travelled to Spain twice in 2001–02 for training in the operation of a lathe acquired through the network. Possibly related to this was an investigation launched by Spain in June 2003 into allegations that Spanish firms had exported high-precision machinery and equipment to Libya for its nuclear programme.[99] Furthermore, the Libyan authorities informed the IAEA in 2004 that during a training visit to another African country, possibly South Africa, its engineers examined a complete set of supporting equipment for 10,000 centrifuges that it ordered from the network.[100]

Through the A.Q. Khan network the Libyan regime was able to gain not only logistical but also technical assistance in its pursuit of nuclear weapons. The question remains as to whether the regime was able to translate these considerable acquisitions into achievements.

Gas centrifuges

From 1997 to 2002, as a direct result of the A.Q. Khan network, Libya progressed significantly further in the centrifuge field than it had been able to over the preceding 20 years. However, it could be argued that, in practice, the advances in its centrifuge programme following the infusions of equipment from the network did not quite fulfil the potential that they signified for it on paper.

The two types of centrifuges acquired from the network by Libya carried the designations L-1 (or G-1 or P-1) and L-2 (or G-2 or P-2). The more basic L-1 design incorporated aluminium rotors while the more advanced L-2 design included rotors manufactured from maraging steel. Khan had allegedly acquired blueprints for both centrifuge designs while working for the Urenco enrichment consortium in Europe, and they were subsequently used in the Pakistani nuclear programme.[101]

The focal point of Libya's centrifuge research and development activities during this period was a facility at Al Hashan on the outskirts of Tripoli (labelled Site A by the IAEA). It was here that work was performed on L-1 centrifuges procured directly from Pakistan, and Libyan scientists and technicians were trained. The acquisition of L-1 centrifuges associated with the Al Hashan facility began shortly after Libya's initial contact with Khan in 1997. This procurement also included systems for process gas feeding and withdrawal as well as frequency converters. A total of 20 complete L-1 centrifuge machines were received from Pakistan, as well as most of the components (except the magnets and aluminium rotors) for another 200. The 20 machines appear to have been retired from Pakistan's centrifuge programme, while other components and equipment were acquired under contract from elsewhere in the network.[102] By October 2000, the Libyans had succeeded in installing and conducting the first test of a single complete centrifuge at Al Hashan using one of the pre-assembled rotors.[103] Two successful high-speed tests of L-1 machines were subsequently performed between May and December 2002, although Libya has claimed that no nuclear material was used.[104]

According to the IAEA, the Libyans had begun installing several centrifuge cascades in a large hall at Al Hashan by late 2000. By April 2002, one nine-machine cascade had reportedly been completed and was under vacuum with all the pipes, electrical connections and process equipment set up. Moreover, a 19-machine cascade was at a similar state of completion with 10 rotors installed, but not under vacuum. Finally, a 64-machine cascade and the associated process equipment were in position and ready for installation, and the mechanical equipment used to test the single centrifuge had also been relocated there.[105] However, the installation work at Al Hashan was completely disrupted in the spring of 2002 when the Libyan authorities decided for security reasons to dismantle the cascades, to pack the components and to move them to Al Fallah (Site B).[106]

Environmental samples taken by the IAEA at Al Hashan in 2004 revealed low-enriched uranium (LEU) and highly enriched uranium (HEU) contamination on the floor of the L-1 test area, on centrifuge and crashed rotor parts, on feed and take-off systems and on a mass spectrometer used during the tests. It has since emerged that at least one of the L-1 casings used for mechanical testing had been in service in Pakistan until 1987 and that most of the contamination was similar to that found in the supplier state.[107] However, ElBaradei informed the IAEA Board of Governors in June 2004 that questions remained about the source of contamination on Libya's centrifuge equipment.[108]

In addition to acquiring L-1 centrifuges, Libya also procured two complete and more advanced L-2 machines directly from Pakistan in September 2000 via the A.Q. Khan network.[109] However, the two machines were not in a workable condition. One of the two 'demonstration models' was unsuitable for actual uranium enrichment because it did not have the final surface coating required to prevent corrosion by UF_6.[110] Libya informed the IAEA in 2004 that 10,000 additional L-2 centrifuges had been ordered and that initial deliveries of components began arriving in December 2002 from elsewhere through the network.[111] The IAEA determined that the two complete L-2 machines were contaminated with HEU, as were some of the L-2 components, presumably as a result of their earlier use in Pakistan.[112]

By the end of 2003, the Gadhafi regime had acquired a significant number of L-2 components, but these did not constitute complete machines because no rotating parts had been delivered. Indeed, IAEA inspectors found the components unopened in boxes in January 2004, which appears to validate Libya's assertion that no L-2 machines had been assembled or tested.[113] Moreover, some of the components received from the network were scratched and therefore not usable.

For his part, Khan has claimed that there was no 'official' Pakistani involvement in the illicit transfers conducted by his network.[114] President Pervez Musharraf has also stated that Khan and his associates worked on their own for profit and were not authorised by the government in any way. According to American officials, for example, Pakistani scientists received payments from Libya alone amounting to as much as US$100m beginning in the 1990s.[115] Nevertheless, it has been speculated that Khan's official pardon in February 2004 was a *quid pro quo* for admitting sole responsibility for the proliferation network and not implicating the government in any way.[116] Given the nature and scale of the nuclear-related transfers to countries like Libya and Iran, it is certainly difficult to imagine them occurring without the consent, or at least the tacit support and knowledge, of wider officialdom, including Pakistan's Inter-Service Intelligence.

In addition to acquiring centrifuges and their related components, the Gadhafi regime sought to obtain the capability to produce such items domestically. The main focus of this effort was a machine shop (Project 1001) located at Janzour (labelled Site E by the IAEA).[117] The Libyans reportedly commissioned the A.Q. Khan network to plan, set up and procure some of the equipment – such as flow-forming machines and lathes – for the workshop.[118] According to one report, Libya's plan was to use the workshop to replace broken imported centrifuges and potentially to increase its total number of machines.[119] When IAEA investigators visited the workshop in 2004 the equipment was still stored in crates. The Libyan authorities informed the IAEA that they had procured a large stock of maraging steel and high-strength aluminium, which can be used in the manufacture of centrifuges. The deal for this transfer apparently included Libyan staff being trained overseas on at least three occasions, although it is not clear where this would have taken place.[120]

Uranium conversion and the import of UF$_6$

Similar to the preceding phase of the nuclear programme, Libya failed completely in its efforts to produce UF$_6$ domestically from the late 1990s until late 2003. Nevertheless, in 1998 most of the modules of the UCF acquired in the 1980s were evacuated to the Al Khalla (Site C) suburb of Tripoli. Here the equipment was assembled and some cold testing of the modules occurred in early 2002, but without any uranium feedstock, before later being moved again for 'reasons of security and secrecy' to the Salah Eddin (Site D) suburb. Environmental sampling performed by the IAEA in 2004 on the surfaces of UCF components confirmed the absence of uranium traces.[121]

Libya's failure to produce UF$_6$ domestically obviously influenced its request to import such material from the Khan network. Indeed, Libya originally asked the network for 20 tonnes of UF$_6$ although it only received three cylinders: two small cylinders were received in September 2000 and one large one in February 2001. The large cylinder contained some 1.7 tonnes of LEU (enriched to around 1% U^{235}) while the other two contained natural and depleted uranium.[122] Uranium enriched to 90% or more, U^{235} is required for the manufacture of nuclear weapons.

The original source of the UF$_6$ has been the subject of much debate and it appears that Libya itself did not know its origin.[123] One view is that North Korea was the original source. The A.Q. Khan network reportedly arranged for the material to be shipped via a Pakistani company and through Dubai to Libya, although there is no evidence that Pyongyang knew the ultimate destination.[124] Analysis of the UF_6 conducted in the United States in 2004 has reportedly pointed the finger at North Korea. In February 2005, it was reported that extensive testing at Oak Ridge National Laboratory led to the conclusion that, 'with near certainty', North Korea was the original source. However, this analysis was constrained by the lack of known samples of North Korean uranium to allow for comparative analysis. The 'near certainty' of the analysis was reportedly reached by eliminating other possible sources. Unsurprisingly, the potential involvement of Pyongyang has been the subject of intense scrutiny and conjecture, partially because if proved to be correct then it would confirm its possession of a uranium-enrichment programme.[125]

Weapon designs

At the end of 2001 and in early 2002, the A.Q. Khan network provided Libya with design and fabrication documentation relating to nuclear weapons which was subsequently stored by the NBSR. The information reportedly included assembly drawings and manufacturing instructions for the components of the 'physics package' – the explosive part of the weapon including the detonator explosives and fissile material, but not the associated electronics and firing sets. They reportedly included the step-by-step process for casting uranium metal into a bomb core and building the explosive lenses that compress the core to initiate a nuclear chain reaction.[126] It has been widely reported that the designs and instructions were for a 10-kilotonne implosion device, following a late 1960s Chinese design and weighing some 453kg. The design had been provided initially to Pakistan and the device was designed for delivery by aircraft or large ballistic missile.[127]

Libya reportedly spent US\$20–50m on the designs.[128] However, one drawing of a key part was reportedly not included in the design and fabrication information, and it is unclear why this was withheld by the network. Moreover, the Gadhafi regime has claimed that no efforts had been taken to assess the utility of the information.[129] This claim appears to be supported by the IAEA, which did not pinpoint specific facilities during inspections in Libya related to the design, manufacture or testing of weapon components.[130] Indeed, those facilities with equipment that could potentially have been utilised in a weapons programme did not have 'dedicated nuclear weapon component production capability'.[131]

Conclusion

By the time the Gadhafi regime opted to abandon its nuclear aspirations in December 2003, Libya had procured most of the technical pieces of the nuclear-weapon jigsaw. However, despite spending millions of dollars purchasing 'off-the-shelf' centrifuge equipment, UF_6 and detailed information on weapon fabrication, Libya had not stockpiled or even produced any weapons-grade uranium, let alone manufactured nuclear warheads.[132] This failure to make significant progress is explained by several factors. At one level, the nuclear programme was evidently not well managed. For example, it is unclear why Libya sought to acquire a workshop for manufacturing centrifuges when it proved to be so straightforward to purchase thousands of completed centrifuges from the Khan network. Poor management may, to an extent, have been the result of a lack of political continuity accorded to the programme over the years.

Perhaps the most significant factor that prevented Libya's nuclear weapons programme from advancing further was the absence of a high-technology industrial and scientific base and associated education system, all of which contributed to a dearth of requisite local expertise in key areas such as centrifuges. So, while the regime focused on buying the technical pieces of the jigsaw, its failure to develop the necessary scientific and technical training programmes meant that it faced a major problem in finding Libyans to assemble the puzzle. Libya has claimed that 800 nuclear specialists were involved in the programme and 140 of these had advanced degrees; some of the senior personnel had been educated in the United States, the United Kingdom and elsewhere in Europe.[133] However, it appears that Libya had only a handful of scientists of international class specialising in nuclear science and engineering. Indeed, Ambassador Donald Mahley, the senior US WMD representative in Libya in early 2004, has noted that while he interacted with 'knowledgeable, dedicated and innovative' individuals in the nuclear field in Libya, he dealt with the same people repeatedly because of what he described as the Libyans having 'almost no bench'.[134] The lack of a suitable domestic infrastructure and local expertise was compounded by the general unwillingness of most countries to trade in sensitive technology with Libya and the constraining effect of multilateral sanctions imposed from 1992.

While the A.Q. Khan network did present a significant opportunity in terms of clandestine procurement, and this was pivotal to pushing forward the programme, the Libyan experience highlights the importance of not automatically equating the ability to buy parts and materials with the capability to establish an effective nuclear-weapon programme.[135]

Moreover, the network did not prove to be a reliable supplier of high-quality materials, equipment and components. For example, the network did not fulfil Libya's request for 20 tonnes of UF_6; the two complete L-2 machines were not delivered in a workable condition; key components were missing from the additional 10,000 L-2 units ordered by Libya; some of the parts delivered for the L-2 were damaged and therefore unusable; and it appears that key information related to weapon design was withheld. Ultimately, Libya's reliance on the A.Q. Khan network reflected the regime's limited procurement options given the significant constraints imposed by the international embargo. As Mahley notes, this clandestine approach to technology acquisition required the Libyans to pay 'sums far in excess of the "fair market value"' for the materials involved and which were 'not very advanced'.[136]

CHAPTER THREE

The Decision

Libya's decision to abandon its nuclear project was the direct result of secret negotiations conducted by the governments of Libya, the United Kingdom and the United States. The decision itself has been the subject of much speculation, with some divergence of opinion over the relative weighting accorded to contributory factors. Issues that have been highlighted include the Gadhafi regime's desire to end sanctions by re-engaging with the United States and the wider international community, the contribution of quiet diplomacy and negotiation, the effect of the toppling of Saddam Hussein, and the intelligence-led interception of nuclear-related technology en route to Libya via the A.Q. Khan network.

This chapter examines the regime's decision to forego the nuclear option and begins by examining the 'official' views put forward by the three governments directly involved in the negotiations. While these views have much in common, they place differing emphases on various factors. Nevertheless, from these it is possible to identify several issues worthy of deeper analysis. Ultimately, the key aspect of the Libyan case was the self-serving nature of the decision dictated by the core interests of the regime.

Initial views

How, then, did the three governments officially portray Libya's decision to give up its pursuit of nuclear weapons? How did their initial views diverge and in what areas?

The Libyan perspective

From various statements by Gadhafi, his eldest son and potential heir Saef al-Islam, and various senior Libyan representatives, it is evident that the regime's official position comprised several elements. Central to this position was the perception that the pursuit and possession of WMD was no longer in line with the regime's security interests.

The official statement from Tripoli announcing the decision noted that Libya 'believes that the arms race will neither serve its security nor the region's security and contradicts its great concern for a world that enjoys peace and security'.[1] Libya's communiqué to the UN Security Council, made public on 23 December 2003, similarly noted that, 'the arms race is conducive neither to its own security nor to that of the region and runs counter to its strong desire for a world blessed with security and peace'.[2]

In an address to the African Union in March 2004, the Libyan leader stated that 'the security of Libya does not come from the nuclear bomb; the nuclear bomb represents a danger to the country which has [it]'.[3] Saef al-Islam also highlighted the importance of security as a driver of the decision. In an interview he noted that Libya was actually 'safer without those items'.[4] Saef al-Islam has also implied that Libya had been developing WMD for use in the event of a conflict with Israel, but that progress in the Israel–Palestinian peace process had 'made such planning unnecessary'.[5]

While security was evidently a key driver of the decision to disarm, the regime was anxious to depict the decision as a Libyan initiative developed of its own free will. In this respect, there were apparently concerns that Libya should not be seen, especially in the Arab world, as having given in to external pressure and the coercive effect of the Iraq War in early 2003. Senior regime members sought to paint a picture of the WMD decision as part of a more general change of political course initiated to reflect the altered international security environment.

On a visit to Brussels to meet senior EU officials in April 2004, Gadhafi noted that while Libya once led the liberation movement in the Third World and Africa, it 'now has decided to lead the peace movement all over the world' and that 'the first step to prove that [the decision to give up WMD] was taken voluntarily'.[6] This inference of a broader policy change was reiterated by Foreign Minister Abdul Rahman Shalgam during a visit to London in February 2004 when he stated that 'things have changed' and 'We have the courage to review our politics and directions. The caravan is moving on.'[7] Indeed, several regime members, including Gadhafi himself, voiced the hope that Libya's actions would serve as a model for other countries to follow, beginning with those in the Middle East.[8]

With specific reference to the Iraq War, Shalgam claimed that Libya had not been scared into action by the use of force against the Saddam Hussein regime, arguing that any suggestions to the contrary were spread by 'malevolent journalists' and Libya's Arab enemies.[9] On this point, Shalgam noted that Libya had been in periodic, and well-documented, talks with the United States dating back as far as 1992. To bolster the argument that Libya had acted of its own accord, he emphasised that the decision would be subject to international 'verification' and not 'inspections', an obvious attempt to differentiate his country's position from that of Iraq, which had been subject to UN weapons inspections prior to the invasion in 2003. Saef al-Islam also claimed the decision had nothing to do with the war, telling CNN that negotiations had started 'before even the invasion of Iraq' and that the decision was not taken 'because we are afraid' or under 'American pressure or blackmail'.[10]

In addition to the security rationale and the claims to have acted voluntarily, statements by senior Libyans also highlighted socio-economic factors in the decision-making process. A recurrent theme proposed by several Libyan representatives was the detrimental impact that the pursuit of WMD had had on the country's economic and social development, and the importance of normalising relations with the United States and Europe for Libya's future development.

At the closing session of the African Union Summit in March 2004, Gadhafi stated that 'the nuclear arms race is a crazy and destructive policy for economy and life'.[11] Moreover, Shalgam told Al Jazeera shortly after the WMD decision was announced that Libya gave them up 'to concentrate on development projects and normalizing relations with the US' and European governments. In doing so, he noted that the programmes did not benefit the people of Libya.[12] Moreover, Saef al-Islam told *al-Hayat* on 10 March 2004 that Libya had taken the decision for 'political, economic, cultural and military gains', underlining the seemingly multivariate factors that contributed to the decision to forego WMD.[13]

The British perspective

The British government's public reaction to Libya's announcement emphasised the role of diplomacy and negotiation. On 19 December 2003, Prime Minister Tony Blair said, 'It shows that problems of proliferation can, with good will, be tackled through discussion and engagement, to be followed up by the responsible international agencies. It demonstrates that countries can abandon programmes voluntarily and peacefully.' In an obvious reference to the war in Iraq, which had been conducted from a British standpoint on

WMD-disarmament grounds, he also commented that Libya 'shows that we can fight this menace through more than purely military means'.[14] For his part, Foreign Secretary Jack Straw noted that the United Kingdom had been engaged in diplomacy with Libya 'going back for six or seven years'.[15] Straw stated that he would not 'claim any crude connection... between military action in Iraq and what has happened in Iraq and in Libya'.[16]

The American perspective

While the official American perspective acknowledged the importance of diplomacy and Libya's desire to rejoin the international community, it emphasised the contribution of the Bush administration's national security strategy, particularly its robust approach to countering proliferation. The 'demonstration effect' of the Iraq war and the US-led PSI were singled out as particular contributory factors. For example, while President Bush noted that the 'understanding with Libya' had come about 'through quiet diplomacy'[17], the official White House response stated that:

> Libya's announcement today is a product of the President's strategy which gives regimes a choice. They can choose to pursue WMD at great peril, cost and international isolation. Or they can choose to renounce these weapons, take steps to rejoin the international community, and have our help in creating a better future for their citizens.

The official response went on to note that the decision was a product of America's determination over the preceding two years following 11 September 2001 'to work in partnership with our allies to combat the nexus of terrorism and WMD'. In doing so, the administration drew attention to the enforcement of UN resolutions to disarm Iraq, the removal of the Taliban regime in Afghanistan and the interdiction of dangerous WMD shipments under the PSI, among other things. In claiming the success of its counter-proliferation strategy in relation to Libya, the Bush administration also sought to send messages to other regimes possessing or contemplating the acquisition of WMD. In this respect, the White House noted that:

> These actions have sent an unmistakable message to regimes that seek or possess WMD: these weapons do not bring influence or prestige – they only bring isolation and other unwelcome consequences. When leaders make the wise and reasonable choice to renounce terror and WMD, they serve the interests of their own people and add to the security of all nations.

The prospect of improved relations with the United States, and the international community as a whole, was also held out as a specific incentive to such states.[18]

Paula A. DeSutter, assistant secretary of verification and compliance at the State Department, highlighted similar issues during her testimony to Congress in February and September 2004. On 22 September, DeSutter stated that:

> It was clear to Gadhafi that we were willing to use all the tools at our disposal to stem the flow of WMD. Ongoing international diplomacy, coupled with economic sanctions, isolated Libya and were having a significant impact on Libya's international status and economy. The Bush adminstration's relentless pursuit of the WMD black market exposed Libya's and other[s'] WMD programs, and diminished their chances of success. It is also indisputable that the example of Iraq was there for all to see. The timing is instructive. In March 2003, as we were getting ready to invade Iraq, the Libyans made their first overtures, but fell short of admitting their nuclear weapon program. In October, after we and our allies in the PSI seized the shipment for Tripoli, Libya permitted the first Americans into the country and made the admission that ultimately ended their programs.[19]

In short, Washington sought to paint a picture of Libya's decision that vindicated the Bush administration's strategy for countering WMD proliferation, including the decision to go to war in Iraq to topple the Saddam Hussein regime and the emphasis placed on pre-emption in its post-9/11 national security strategy. Douglas Feith, then under secretary of defense, reportedly referred directly to the demonstration effect of US policy, claiming that Gadhafi's decision was due to the sobering effect of the American-led ousting of the Taliban and Saddam regimes in Afghanistan and Iraq, respectively.[20]

Drawing on these official views, it is possible to single out several issues that, if explored further, might shed light on the decision to disarm. The first, and most important, is Libya's change of political trajectory during the 1990s.

Libya's change of political trajectory

One seasoned Libya-watcher has observed that the decision to disarm was primarily the result of 'a lengthy, systematic process' initiated in the early 1990s to bring the country in from the cold.[21] The process appears to have begun just before multilateral UN sanctions were imposed on Libya in 1992. Over the next decade or so the regime made incremental, but ultimately wholesale, changes to both the rhetoric and practice of its external relations. These changes contrasted starkly with the hostile and defiant approach adopted by the regime towards the outside world over much of the preceding two decades. Libya's change of political trajectory was characterised most notably by the regime's termination of support for international terrorism, its gradual but eventually full cooperation with the British and American governments in resolving the Lockerbie case, and Gadhafi's reorientation of Libya's external relations away from pan-Arabism towards pan-Africanism. Ultimately, it was this trajectory that created the political context within which Libya chose to relinquish the pursuit of nuclear and chemical weapons. What, then, prompted these changes on the part of the Gadhafi regime?

Multilateral pressure grows

In the latter half of 1991, after months of mounting international pressure on Libya to cooperate with the Lockerbie investigations, and as the prospect of multilateral sanctions loomed ever larger, the rhetoric of the Gadhafi regime began to change. In December, the regime announced that it would sever relations with organisations involved in terrorist activities, although it went no further in responding on Lockerbie.[22] Consequently, on 21 January 1992, the UN Security Council passed Resolution 731, which called on Tripoli to hand-over the two Libyan officials charged with the bombing; to accept responsibility for their actions; to pay adequate compensation; to renounce terrorism and to demonstrate this through its actions; and to provide all the information that it held on Lockerbie. Libya was also called upon to cooperate with the French investigation into the downing of flight UTA 772 in 1989.

The lack of an adequate response resulted in Resolution 748 on 31 March 1992, which imposed a ban on all flights to and from Libya until the suspects were handed over to British or American authorities. The continued failure to cooperate resulted in Resolution 883 of 11 November 1993, which strengthened the sanctions further by banning sales of oil equipment to Libya and implementing a freeze on several billion US dollars' worth of the country's foreign assets.[23] Prohibitions were placed on the transfer to Libya of 'specific items used for transporting oil and natural gas'.[24] Resolutions 748 and 883 also prohibited exports to Libya that could be used to develop WMD or to enhance its conventional military capabilities.[25]

The UN sanctions were designed to be 'targeted' in their effect and not to 'cripple' the country's economy. Moreover, while the UN embargo was not as comprehensive as America's unilateral sanctions, it constituted a major problem for Tripoli because its universality promised to constrain significantly the regime's ability to bolster trade with other states legitimately.[26] Libya's virtually complete dependence on oil for its export earnings was by far the regime's biggest economic vulnerability. Approximately 99% of Libya's export earnings are derived from oil, although the industry itself only employs some 10% of the country's workforce.[27]

For reasons of economic self interest, many European governments had opposed the imposition of comprehensive UN sanctions and a complete oil embargo. It has been estimated that some 95% of Libya's oil exports go to Europe, with Germany and Italy highly reliant on Libya's light crude for their refineries.[28] Libya was the biggest supplier to both countries each year during the period from 1991 to 2004.[29] Moreover, the European Union was the destination of some 85% of exports from Libya during the 1990s (Germany, Italy and Spain reportedly accounted for some 80% of this amount) and also provided some 75% of its imports.[30]

In an effort to strengthen the international embargo on Libya, and in the face of strong European opposition, US President Bill Clinton signed into law the Congressionally inspired Iran–Libya Sanctions Act (ILSA) in August 1996. The ILSA provided for the imposition of mandatory US sanctions on foreign companies that made investments contributing directly and significantly to the development of petroleum or natural gas resources in Iran and Libya.[31] While the legislation was originally designed with Iran in mind, Congress had supported an amendment which applied its provisions to Libya in an effort to increase the pressure on Tripoli to give up the Lockerbie suspects. Specifically, the ILSA required the United States to impose sanctions on foreign companies that invested over US$40m over a period of 12 months in Libya's energy sector. If the president could determine that Libya had fulfilled the requirements laid out by the Security Council then the ILSA would no longer be enforceable for this country.[32]

Unsurprisingly, the EU opposed the ILSA on the grounds that it constituted the extra-territorial application of American law. As a result of European pressure the Clinton administration agreed to waive sanctions on the first deal deemed to violate the provisions of the ILSA – a contract worth US$2bn for France's Total SA to develop Iran's South Pars gas field.[33] Other entities, such as Italy's ENI (National Hydrocarbons Agency), were also later granted waivers.[34] In effect, European commercial interests undermined America's quest for a more comprehensive multilateral sanctions regime for Libya.[35] Nevertheless, the EU countries did on the whole adhere to the multilateral sanctions targeted at Libya. One example involved not allowing Libya to participate in the EU-sponsored Euro-Mediterranean partnership process initiated in Barcelona in 1995.[36]

The sanctions effect

The combined effect of the unilateral American embargo and multilateral UN sanctions had a significant impact on Libya's economy. In turn, this generated problems that threatened to undermine the security of the Gadhafi regime.

During the 1970s and into the 1980s the Libyan regime had exploited revenues generated by the oil boom to help to secure and maintain domestic popular support.[37] This was done through the establishment and maintenance of an impressive welfare and education system and by providing employment through an extensive public sector. Moreover, every Libyan national and legal immigrant was entitled to have access to housing, healthcare, food, water and electricity, and the state even provided its citizens with a car paid for by installments.[38] However, declining oil prices in the 1980s and 1990s, combined with the impact of UN sanctions on the importation of oil equipment, subsequently constrained the country's oil exports and reduced state revenues.[39] The situation was exacerbated because Libya's oil industry was based on American technology and equipment. According to Hammouda el-Aswad, the head of Libya's National Oil Corporation (NOC), interviewed in 1999, the United States had placed every piece of equipment on its unilateral sanctions list in 1986. In 1992, the imposition of multilateral sanctions meant that Libya could no longer legally purchase oil equipment on the open market.[40]

The dissuasive effect of the ILSA on non-American companies investing and working in Libya further restricted the effective operation of the country's oil sector. Cumulatively, then, American and subsequently UN sanctions significantly limited oil exploration and expansion in Libya.[41] Levels of Libyan oil production in the 1970s were twice those of 2003.[42]

The combination of significantly lower oil revenues, and the inability to expand oil production due to the embargoes, contributed to a general economic malaise. The state's ineffective socialist-based economic planning and controls, the oversized public sector and the Gadhafi regime's opposition to foreign ownership all exacerbated Libya's economic problems. In terms of gross domestic product, Libya went from a position of general parity with the United Arab Emirates in 1982 to the situation in 2003 where its GDP was one-seventh of that of the Gulf state.[43] This was despite the fact that Libya possesses significant unexploited oil resources, with only a reported quarter of the country so far prospected.[44]

The drop in oil income led to a significant reduction in public spending because 75% of government revenue was derived from oil exports.[45] As a result, public sector pay remained effectively frozen from 1982 through to 2003, although inflation continued to grow over the same period (some 60% of state expenditure in Libya is reported to have been allocated to paying wages).[46] Moreover, the state sector could no longer incorporate all those people seeking work, which resulted in growing unemployment. By 2003, the unemployment rate in Libya was approximately 25% and the workforce was growing by 4% every 12 months.[47]

The resultant decline in living standards contributed to growing dissatisfaction with the Libyan state, which became increasingly less capable of fulfilling basic needs and expectations. Growing popular discontent saw the regime confronted by a burgeoning younger generation experiencing high levels of unemployment and increasingly alienated from the political process and, therefore, susceptible to the attraction of opposition groups.[48]

The Muslim Brotherhood was one movement of particular concern for the Gadhafi regime because it espoused economic and political reforms in line with Islamic ideals. The country's economic malaise made the Brotherhood's agenda an attractive option to many blue-collar workers, traders and junior civil servants. The movement's social welfare programmes were particularly appealing to urban and poor populations. Another opposition grouping was the National Salvation Front, a broad-based opposition movement that sought to develop a platform accommodating secular and Islamic opponents.[49]

The regime also experienced a major growth in violence targeted against the state during the mid-1990s, initiated by militant Islamist groups. The violence ranged from clashes with security forces to an attempt to assassinate Gadhafi himself in August 1995. The violence illustrated the increasing popular dissatisfaction with the regime's political oppression and economic mismanagement. It also demonstrated that Islamist insurgents were capable of threatening the regime's security apparatus and potentially, therefore, its hold on power. Islamist opposition groups that supported armed resistance included the Islamic Liberation Party (ILP) and the Islamic Martyrdom Movement (IMM). While the ILP had developed links with student movements and also within the army, the IMM recruited from Libyan returnees from the conflict in Afghanistan who had 'limited means of subsistence'.[50] Another group, the Libyan Islamic Fighting Force, was allegedly linked to Osama bin Laden's al-Qaeda network.[51]

In summary, the combined effect of sanctions, international isolation and the state's failure to manage the economy created a domestic environment in which political dissent increased, boosting support for opposition groups. This situation posed a significant and growing problem for Gadhafi and presented him with the challenge of improving Libya's economic situation and political standing. Priority was placed on modernising and expanding the oil sector, and re-invigorating the stagnant economy by increasing foreign investment. This necessitated taking steps to end the UN and American embargoes and, ultimately, to re-engage with the international community, particularly with the United States. Indeed, as early as the spring of 1992, following the imposition of the first UN sanctions, the regime reportedly established a 'high-level committee' specifically tasked with re-opening communications with Washington.[52]

Declining support for terrorism and cooperation over Lockerbie

The most significant development was the regime's changing position on terrorism, which involved a dramatic reduction in Libya's support for terrorist groups and activities. The State Department noted in 2002 that there had been 'no credible reports of Libyan involvement in terrorism since 1994'.[53] It was also noted in 2003 that 'close official and independent observers of Libyan behavior are hard-pressed to find evidence of terrorist involvement in the last decade'.[54] Libya's apparent exit from the terrorism business during the 1990s was directly in line with demands set out in Resolution 731.

After a period of stalemate over the Lockerbie issue, in August 1998 the Gadhafi regime accepted a UK–US proposal to put the suspects on trial in the Netherlands under Scottish law. In response, the Security Council passed Resolution 1192 calling for the suspension of sanctions once the suspects were handed over, which occurred in April 1999.[55] These developments were perceived by many Western officials and observers as proof that targeted and tightly enforced multilateral sanctions, and international isolation, could be successfully applied to coerce wayward regimes into moderating their policies and actions.[56] In terms of economic pressure, Libya claimed that the UN sanctions had cost the regime US$26.5bn in 'real and imputed costs' between 1992–3 and 2001.[57] The decision to hand over the suspects was also facilitated by Gadhafi's success in constraining political opposition to his regime within the army, tribal groups and militant Islamist movements by the end of the 1990s.[58]

The Lockerbie decision signalled a sea-change in the regime's external relations and brought about the possibility of restoring economic and political links with the wider world. Although the multilateral embargo was suspended, American sanctions remained in place and the complete removal of UN sanctions depended on Libya's continued cooperation with the Lockerbie and UTA investigations. In the event, Libya's *volte face* on terrorism persisted. For example, in 1999 Gadhafi expelled the ANO and its members from Libya.[59] Moreover, Gadhafi evidently shared the anxieties of other countries in the region about Islamist militants, including those associated with the al-Qaeda network.[60] For this reason, Libya began cooperating with Egypt, Jordan and Yemen on counter-terrorism issues.[61] Following the terrorist attacks of 11 September 2001, Gadhafi also made anti-terrorist statements and began providing intelligence on al-Qaeda to the United States.

In line with its declining support for terrorism, Gadhafi also began expressing support for the Middle East peace process during the 1990s. Despite its continued anti-Israeli rhetoric, the regime began to support the new Palestinian Authority and, in doing so, withdrew its backing from the more radical Palestinian organisations, including the ANO and Palestinian Islamic Jihad.[62]

Pan-Africanism versus pan-Arabism

Another element of Gadhafi's altered political trajectory involved developing relations with various African governments.[63] This occurred in parallel with Libya's disengagement from the Arab world, which had been such a focal point for the regime during its Arab nationalist heydays in the 1970s and 1980s.[64] The regime had resented the lack of Arab support for breaching the embargo on Libya, including the ban on flights to and from the country.[65]

The very public shift in focus, and Libya's promotion of cooperation among African states, reflected Gadhafi's desire to re-establish himself as a player on the international stage.[66] Moreover, Libya's active engagement with other African states was designed primarily to generate allies in the quest to remove UN sanctions completely.[67] By the end of 1997, the multilateral embargo had begun to show signs of strain, with African leaders taking the lead in opposing sanctions.[68] Libya's provision of financial aid certainly played a role in garnering the support of African governments. For example, Libya paid the budget contribution arrears for 11 Organisation of African Unity (OAU) member states during the 2001–02 financial year.[69] In June 1998, the OAU threatened to ignore the sanctions if the Lockerbie issue was not resolved within three months. It has been argued that this threat was enough to prompt the British and American governments to accept the hand-over of the suspects for trial in The Hague.[70]

Gadhafi became particularly active in promoting pan-Africanism after UN sanctions were suspended in 1999. In August he proposed the establishment of a United States of Africa to include an African central bank and a focus on development. Gadhafi also subsequently proposed setting up an African court, army and legislature. Moreover, following the replacement of the OAU with the African Union in 2002, Libya became one of its largest financial donors.[71]

Domestic reforms

In addition to changing course at the international level, Gadhafi initiated domestic reforms following the suspension of UN sanctions, including the decision in March 2000 to dissolve the ministries responsible for agriculture, education, health, housing, mining, planning, telecommunications and transport, and to reassign responsibility in these areas to local councils.[72] This move was designed to deflect the blame for Libya's problems away from Gadhafi himself and on to the 'state'; the suspension of UN sanctions meant that the regime could no longer claim that the outside world was the cause of the country's problems.[73]

While these initial reforms appeared designed to direct criticism away from Gadhafi, the regime announced in June 2003 that the country's long experimentation with socialism and state planning had failed, and that the public sector was to be dismantled and 'the economy liberalised'.[74] The former trade and economy minister, Harvard-educated Shukri Muhammad Ghanem, was appointed prime minister and instructed to start pushing through the changes. A proponent of privatisation and foreign investment, Ghanem announced in October 2003 a list of 361 companies in the agricultural, cement, petrochemical, steel and other sectors to be privatised in 2004.[75] The regime thus began to abandon its long-standing opposition to the foreign ownership of Libyan assets.[76]

During the 1990s and the first years of the twenty-first century, the Gadhafi regime made incremental, but ultimately wholesale, changes to its external relations. It is against this backdrop that Libya's decision to forego WMD must be considered.

Diplomacy, secret negotiations and the nuclear end-game

While Libya succeeded in having UN sanctions suspended in 1999, it took another four years before they were completely removed. Ultimately, this required full compliance with the demands that the Security Council had set out in 1992. It took a further 12 months before US sanctions were removed, which required the regime to give up verifiably the pursuit of nuclear and chemical weapons. Libya's decision on WMD was essentially part of a much broader continuum of engagement which the Gadhafi regime initiated during the late 1990s. Moreover, quiet diplomacy and secret negotiations involving the Libyan, British and American governments proved to be pivotal to achieving progress on this front.

While the decision was not announced until December 2003, the Gadhafi regime had already demonstrated potential readiness effectively to trade in its WMD option to avoid sanctions in the early 1990s. As part of Libya's attempts to reopen communications with the United States in early 1992, the regime sought to engage diplomatically with Washington by reaching out on WMD.[77] However, the administration of George H.W. Bush rejected the regime's approaches, opting instead to place an emphasis on Libya complying with UN resolutions before engaging in any dialogue.[78]

On the sidelines of Lockerbie
It was not until the spring of 1999 that the US State Department eventually entered into secret negotiations with the Libyan regime, which laid the groundwork for the eventual resolution of the Lockerbie affair. During the final two years of the Clinton presidency (1999–2000), the US government informed the Gadhafi regime on the sidelines of the Lockerbie negotiations that Libya would have to resolve concerns about its WMD ambitions, and not just terrorism, before the United States would fully accept it back into the international fold. The British government adopted a similar position. In short, resolving Lockerbie alone was not going to be enough.[79]

The British government played a pivotal role in facilitating the secret negotiations that resolved both Lockerbie and eventually also the WMD issue.[80] The Libyans could not approach the United States directly and Britain presented a crucial 'back-channel'. London resumed diplomatic relations with Tripoli in July 1999, after Libya accepted responsibility for the murder of London policewoman Yvonne Fletcher in 1984 and agreed to help to investigate the shooting.[81] Following the resumption of official relations, a British diplomatic presence was quickly re-established in Tripoli, which subsequently proved crucial in bringing the Gadhafi regime in from the cold.

It has been suggested that one motivating factor for the Blair government in its cooperation with the Gadhafi regime was the prospect of participating in the post-sanctions revival of the Libyan economy following the suspension of UN sanctions.[82] Interestingly, Britain had reportedly kept in place 'informal contacts' with Libya during the 15 years prior to 1999, despite officially cutting diplomatic links in 1984.[83] Notably, after the announcement of the WMD decision in December 2003, senior Libyans, including Gadhafi, Saef al-Islam and Ghanem, all credited Britain and Blair with 'doing the most to bring Libya out of isolation'.[84] However, while the British government certainly fulfilled a pivotal role in the secret negotiations, and provided the Libyans with a bridge to the Americans, only the United States had in its gift what the Libyans most sought: an end to American sanctions and reengagement with Washington.[85]

Initial round of negotiations

The initial round of secret negotiations encompassed talks between May 1999 and early 2000 in the United Kingdom and Switzerland. The Libyan negotiators included the Head of External Intelligence Musa Kusa, thereby demonstrating continuity in Libya's interlocutors from the early 1990s.[86] The Clinton administration's Assistant Secretary of State for Near Eastern Affairs, Martin S. Indyk, who initiated the contact for the Americans, warned that the talks would be conditional on them remaining secret and on Tripoli ceasing its efforts to have the sanctions removed, conditions to which the Libyans subsequently agreed.[87] The surrender of the Lockerbie suspects had increased the pressure within the UN for a full removal of the multilateral sanctions, but Washington wanted the entire issue resolved before this happened.[88]

During the talks the Clinton administration focused on resolving the Lockerbie issue, though there was also discussion of cooperation in countering al-Qaeda and other radical Islamist groups. It was on the sidelines of these discussions that the Libyans also demonstrated a willingness to give up the country's chemical weapons programme, to join the Chemical Weapons Convention (CWC), to open its facilities to inspection and to take part in multilateral arms control talks in the Middle East. However, given that the chemical programme was not deemed to pose an immediate threat, and because Washington did not know about the extent of Libya's nuclear weapon programme at this time, resolving Lockerbie remained the priority.[89] Nevertheless, the administration did inform the Gadhafi regime that the removal of American sanctions and further engagement would eventually depend on Libya also addressing WMD. The initial round of talks was suspended in 2000 due to concerns within the Clinton administration about potential leaks during the presidential election on the politically sensitive issue of negotiating with Libya.[90]

Round two

The hiatus in US–Libya negotiations continued through the election of George W. Bush as president. The Bush administration was reportedly nervous about restarting secret talks because of concerns that the families of Lockerbie victims would be angry if they found out that Washington was engaging with Gadhafi before this issue had been fully resolved.[91] Indeed, in

February 2001, Bush and Blair released a joint statement calling on Tripoli to fulfil the requirements of all relevant Security Council resolutions.[92]

Talks with the Gadhafi regime were subsequently resumed, partly as a result of the terrorist attacks of 11 September 2001. From October 2001 through to December 2003 the Bush administration, including Assistant Secretary of State for Near Eastern Affairs William J. Burns, held at least six meetings with the Libyans.[93] The American, British and Libyan governments began to share information on the al-Qaeda network, including affiliated organisations like the Libyan Islamic Fighting Force.[94] According to Flynt Leverett, who worked on Middle East policy in the Bush administration's National Security Council 'during two years of diplomatic negotiations beginning in 2002',[95] the American and British governments communicated to the Libyans that UN sanctions would be permanently removed if they fulfilled Security Council resolutions related to Lockerbie, but that US sanctions would then only be lifted if the WMD issue were addressed.[96] Leverett has also noted that, in order for the United States to pursue a 'more constructive course with Libya', the decision to move forward on the Lockerbie case was approved by 'an informal coalition' consisting of US National Security Advisor Condoleezza Rice and Secretary of State Colin Powell. In doing so, the neo-conservatives in the Department of Defense and the Bureau of Arms Control in the State Department – which opposed offering positive incentives to induce improved behaviour by states of concern – were sidelined 'when crucial decisions were made'.[97]

During the first meeting of the renewed negotiations in London in October 2001, American officials and a Libyan team led by Kusa discussed potential cooperation in the counter-terrorism field.[98] The meeting effectively laid the ground for the final resolution of the Lockerbie issue and, ultimately, it paved the way for the decision on WMD. Indeed, on this latter issue, the Libyan government signed the Comprehensive Test Ban Treaty (CTBT) the following month on the last day of the 'entry into force' conference. Tripoli's delegate stated that Libya 'attaches great importance to questions of disarmament, especially nuclear weapons, and other weapons of mass destruction'.[99] Just two months later, in December 2001, Gadhafi subsequently notified diplomats in The Hague that Libya was prepared to sign the CWC.[100] A further public sign of Libya's changing position on WMD came in November 2002 when it signed the International Code of Conduct Against Ballistic Missile Proliferation.[101]

Detailed negotiations on Lockerbie began under British auspices in 2002 and focused on the issue of compensation, Libya's acceptance of responsibility for the blowing up of Pan Am Flight 103 and broader terrorism issues.[102] The Libyan negotiating team comprised three main interlocutors: Mohammed Zwai, Libya's ambassador to the UK, Abdellati Obaidi, the ambassador to Italy, and Kusa[103]; all were close confidants of the Libyan leader. The breakthrough with Libya was based in part on a back-channel that had been established with a senior Libyan official, assumed to be Kusa, by Britain's Secret Intelligence Service (SIS).[104] Moreover, the earlier resumption of diplomatic relations between the two countries paved the way for Mike O'Brien, the then UK Foreign Office minister responsible for relations with North Africa, to visit Libya in August 2002.[105] During his talks, O'Brien discussed the subject of WMD, among other things, with Gadhafi, and was given 'positive assurances of cooperation over the weapons issue'.[106] This meeting appears to have confirmed to the Libyans that Britain constituted a channel through which Tripoli could potentially deal and negotiate with the United States on WMD. The August trip was followed up in September by Blair personally contacting Gadhafi and asking him to to end Libya's WMD programme.[107] The prime minister's approach was reportedly made with the knowledge of President Bush and Gadhafi is reported to have responded by indicating that his foreign minister had been directed to discuss 'signing conventions' with Britain.[108]

It was not until mid-March 2003, however, that Libya contacted SIS to initiate talks aimed specifically at dismantling WMD programmes in return for removing sanctions and normalising relations.[109] The direct involvement of Saef al-Islam – widely regarded as a representative of his father and potential heir – in this approach was taken as a sign that Gadhafi himself was ready to negotiate on this score. For his part, Saef al-Islam was seen to be a moderating influence on his father and intent on bringing Libya in from the cold by achieving a rapprochement with the West. Under his direction, the Qaddafi International Foundation for Charity Associations also helped to arrange compensation for the families of Lockerbie and UTA victims, which the regime itself claimed did not come from the government. Moreover, the organisation had negotiated hostage releases and arranged ransom payments for the release of Western hostages taken by militants in the Philippines and Algeria, as well as sending relief assistance to other African countries.[110] Interestingly, Saef al-Islam's efforts and role in moderating Libyan foreign policy were reflected in an article he wrote in Spring 2003 on 'Libya–American Relations'. On the final page he noted that 'Libya is now ready to transform decades of mutual antagonism into an era of genuine friendship'. Significantly, the article recognised that WMD had become the final key issue that Tripoli had to address before US–Libya relations could get fully back on track:

> Let me cite one further shadow on the horizon. The UN resolution that serves as the basis of the sanctions against Libya requires renunciation of any future terrorism. As I have made clear, Libya fully complies with that demand. Recently, however, the United States has raised the bar to give the condition a spin it did not have when the resolution was passed. It now holds that the resolution covers weapons of mass destruction as well.[111]

The involvement of Saef al-Islam may have highlighted a further factor underlying both the WMD decision and the resolution of the Lockerbie issues, which were both designed to bring Libya in from the cold: a potential desire to smooth the future succession process by re-engaging with the West and enabling Gadhafi eventually to hand over a stronger country and more stable regime to his successor.

Iraq: the demonstration effect?
Libya's approach to British intelligence on the eve of the US-led war to remove the Saddam regime from power in Iraq has prompted speculation about the influence of the Iraq war on decision-making in Tripoli. While the initial approach occurred just prior to the outbreak of hostilities in the Gulf, British intelligence officers reportedly met Saef al-Islam during the first stage of coalition operations in Iraq.[112] Unsurprisingly, there has been a debate over the potential 'demonstration effect' that forcible regime change in Iraq – on disarmament grounds – may have had on Gadhafi. The Bush administration has been the main proponent of this argument, with various officials painting a picture of the regime's calculations based on a desire to avoid military confrontation with the United States. For example, in an obvious reference to the use of force in Iraq and Libya's subsequent decision on WMD, Bush stated in his January 2004 State of the Union address that 'for diplomacy to be effective, words must be credible, and no one can now doubt the word of America'.[113]

However, Tripoli had been involved in discussions since 1999 with London and Washington, during which the issue of WMD had been touched upon. Moreover, the Gadhafi regime had demonstrated a willingness potentially to negotiate in this area as early as 1992. This earlier activity constituted part of the regime's attempts to re-engage by bargaining away sanctions and isolation. Washington had also made it clear to Tripoli since at least 1999 that the WMD issue would need to be addressed after that of

Lockerbie had been resolved if the United States was to re-engage fully and to lift its unilateral sanctions. This message was first transmitted to Libya before the terrorist attacks of 11 September 2001, the US-led war in Afghanistan to unseat the Taliban and to disrupt and destroy elements of al-Qaeda, the release of the Bush administration's pre-emptive security strategy and the war in Iraq. The Iraq War cannot, therefore, be described as a principal driving factor of Gadhafi's decision to disarm.

Nevertheless, as noted earlier, Gadhafi and various Libyan officials have drawn attention since late 2003 to their perception that the pursuit and possession of WMD was no longer in line with the regime's security interests. These weapons were depicted as bringing insecurity and Libya was perceived to be safer without them. They had become a liability rather than a strategic asset. Moreover, Gadhafi reportedly told Italian Prime Minister Silvio Berlusconi during a phone conversation after Saddam Hussein was toppled that 'I will do whatever the Americans want, because I saw what happened in Iraq, and I was afraid'.[114] Given the timing of the March 2003 approach, it is difficult to discount totally the effect of Iraq on the decision to forego WMD. It appears that the war may have cemented the regime's perception that its interests were best served by cooperating on WMD, and in the process it may have provided added impetus by accelerating the decision to disarm. Ultimately, however, it seems almost certain that the decision would have been made regardless of Iraq because Tripoli knew that resolving WMD constituted the final step to ensuring the removal of US sanctions once Lockerbie had been addressed.

Negotiations move forward

Following Libya's approach on WMD in March 2003, British intelligence officials began meeting and negotiating secretly with Kusa and other Libyans in London and elsewhere. At first, the negotiations only involved the Libyans and British intelligence but they subsequently expanded to include officials from the Foreign and Commonwealth Office and, on the US side, the CIA and the State Department.[115] Throughout their duration the WMD negotiations were the subject of intense secrecy in all three governments, with only a very limited number of officials involved in or aware of the initiative. The secrecy was driven by the desire to avoid any opposition to the initiative developing in Libya, the United States or elsewhere that could potentially have undermined the deal. Ensuring the talks remained a tightly held secret also served to build trust between the three negotiating parties. Within the British government, for example, Blair, Straw and Secretary of State for Defence Geoff Hoon were reportedly the only cabinet members aware of the negotiations.[116] Moreover, within the Bush administration 'in the lead up to the negotiations involving Libyan weapons of mass destruction, the neoconservatives at the Pentagon and in the shop [the Bureau of Arms Control, US State Department] of Under Secretary of State John Bolton were left out of the loop'.[117] British officials 'at the highest level' had reportedly persuaded the White House to keep Bolton away from the Libyan negotiations because of his lack of support for reaching a compromise under which the Bush administration would abandon its goal of regime change in Libya for a verifiable abandonment of its WMD.[118]

The UK and US told the Libyans that they needed to make further concessions on issues related to Lockerbie before progress could be made on WMD.[119] The major breakthrough in this respect occurred on 15 August 2003 when the Libyan government wrote to the Security Council addressing the remaining issues of concern on Lockerbie, including acceptance of responsibility for the actions of Libyan officials and consenting to pay compensation to the Pan Am families.[120] Libya agreed to pay each family up to US$10m: US$4m when UN sanctions were lifted and a further payment when US sanctions were removed. The UK subsequently drafted a resolution to lift the UN sanctions, which the Security Council voted 13–0 to adopt on 12 September.[121] While the United States abstained from the vote, the Bush administration was quick to emphasise that WMD and other issues, such as human rights, remained serious causes for concern.[122] However, in September 2003 the administration initiated what has been described as the equivalent of an 'all-agency review' of America's relations with Libya.[123]

The termination of UN sanctions, as a direct result of a UK-sponsored resolution following the conclusion of the Lockerbie affair, demonstrated to Libya that its negotiating partners could be expected to fulfil their commitments vis-à-vis WMD. In early August, Gadhafi had already stated during an interview on ABC News that he was ready to allow inspections by international organisations, including the IAEA, of industrial sites that could be used in the manufacture of WMD.[124]

The intelligence lever

From a British and American perspective, the priority was to derive a verifiable agreement from Libya's apparent willingness to trade in its programmes. It took some 'considerable prodding' by British intelligence to convince the Libyans to be totally frank about all of their WMD activities.[125] However, progress in this area began to accelerate significantly from late September 2003. A major part of this process involved British and American officials revealing intelligence-derived information to their

Libyan counterparts to demonstrate that they knew what the regime was doing in the WMD field, particularly in the nuclear and missile areas.

Intelligence on the A.Q. Khan network and its relationship with Libya had been uncovered as early as 2000.[126] For example, Britain's Joint Intelligence Committee (JIC) began monitoring the network from early 2000 and quickly established that Libya was probably receiving enrichment equipment from this source. By the summer of 2002, the JIC had determined that the network was 'central to all aspects' of Libya's nuclear weapon programme.[127] The monitoring of this programme evidently represented a major intelligence success for the British and American governments, which stood in contrast to the intelligence failure over Iraq's WMD.

The most well-publicised specific intelligence success involved the interception of centrifuge technology on the German-flagged vessel *BBC China* en route from Dubai to Libya in early October 2003.[128] The origin of the interception was reported to be an intelligence tip in August 2003 on a shipment from the SCOPE factory in Malaysia. The shipment was tracked from Malaysia to the UAE, where crates containing centrifuge components were switched to the *BBC China*. After the vessel was instructed to divert to the port of Taranto in Italy on 4 October, Italian and American officials removed the centrifuge technology.[129]

The interception demonstrated to Tripoli that its negotiating partners had significant and current knowledge about Libya's clandestine nuclear supply network, and it proved the existence of an active gas-centrifuge programme. By placing evidence on the table, Washington and London constrained Libya's room for manoeuvre during the negotiations. The intelligence revelations constituted a 'vital lever' to pressure Libya into admitting its WMD capabilities during trilateral talks that ran from October through to December 2003.[130] The revelations also helped to build trust between the negotiating parties because they demonstrated to the Libyans that their British and American partners trusted them enough to share very sensitive information at a time when the A.Q. Khan network remained under investigation and its existence had yet to be publicly acknowledged.

Following the interception of the *BBC China*, the talks progressed more rapidly. In October and again in December, British and American intelligence officials gained access to some chemical and nuclear sites in Libya and in doing so they acquired first-hand knowledge of the nature and scope of the country's illicit weapons activities.[131] However, while the *BBC China* episode may have accelerated the process, in common with the Iraq War it cannot be described as a pivotal driving factor, given that Libya had long expressed a willingness to forego WMD.[132]

The nuclear end-game

The final act in the negotiations involved diplomatic and intelligence officials from Britain and the United States meeting with their Libyan interlocutors in mid-December. During this meeting in London, Libya agreed to relinquish its chemical and nuclear weapon programmes in return for the ending of US sanctions. It was also agreed that Tripoli's foreign minister would announce that Libya possessed chemical and nuclear weapons programmes and was abandoning them, followed by a public endorsement of the decision by Gadhafi. There was evidently concern that the Libyan regime could potentially renounce WMD but in the process not reveal the full extent of its past and current weapons programmes.[133] As it turned out, of course, this concern proved to be unfounded.

One further intriguing fact was that while Libya had been moderating its behaviour on the international stage, it continued to procure nuclear technology via the A.Q. Khan network. This issue has prompted speculation that the Gadhafi regime may have come to view its nuclear programme as a 'bargaining chip' in its dealings with the United States. This might have reflected Libya's realisation that it was not going to bridge the technical gap in the nuclear arena despite spending millions of dollars on its efforts over more than two decades. As the WMD Intelligence Commission noted in March 2005, 'The lack of sufficient progress in developing a nuclear weapon is one of the factors that may have prompted Gadhafi to abandon and disclose Libya's nuclear program'.[134] Furthermore, trading in the nuclear card for such a major return could have been seen as a face-saving 'get out' measure when comparatively so little had been achieved.

The 'bargaining chip' argument gains at least some credibility when considered in the context of the regime's efforts to use Libya's oil reserves for political and economic leverage. For example, by allowing America's 'Oasis Group' – Conoco-Phillips, Marathon Oil and Amerada Hess[135] – to retain their oil concessions in Libya despite the US embargo (through 'standstill' agreements reserving their right to return), the regime helped to keep up the pressure on Congress and the White House from the mid-1980s.[136] The Bush administration was under great pressure from commercial interests which were lobbying for an end to sanctions.[137] Moreover, the Gadhafi regime increased the pressure during 2001, when it informed American oil companies that they must use their concessions or risk losing them to European companies. In March 2002, Marathon Oil was subsequently informed by the State Department that it could begin discussions with the Libyans before UN and US sanctions were completely lifted.[138]

Conclusion

The decision to disarm was the result of the Gadhafi regime's decade-long quest to end the UN and American embargoes imposed on Libya as a result of its past terrorist-related activities. In this respect, the key aspect of the Libyan case was the self-serving nature of the decision which was driven by the Gadhafi regime's core interests. Sanctions worked in the Libyan context because they targeted the regime's dependency on oil to finance the country's over-sized public sector and discouraged the involvement of foreign companies in the Libyan economy, primarily the oil sector. The outcome was a significant reduction in state revenues, a parallel decline in state expenditure and a rapidly deteriorating economy, which in turn generated political challenges for the regime that threatened to undermine its security. It is against this backdrop that the decision to relinquish the pursuit of nuclear weapons was taken.

Confronted with the challenge of improving Libya's economic situation and strengthening the regime's domestic political position , Gadhafi's overriding priority was to modernise and expand the oil sector and to reinvigorate the stagnant economy by increasing foreign investment. In turn, this necessitated adopting policies and taking steps to end the UN and American embargoes, and ultimately to re-engage with the international community and the United States in particular. The quest to end sanctions involved several important changes in the regime's foreign policy between 1992 and 2003, including its departure from the terrorism business, the hand-over of the Lockerbie suspects and subsequent cooperation to resolve the Lockerbie issue, the re-orientation towards pan-Africanism and, ultimately, the decision to forego its nuclear and chemical programmes and long-range missiles.

From an American and British perspective, the WMD decision was thus part of a much broader engagement with the Gadhafi regime during the late 1990s. The American and British governments made it clear to Tripoli that once the Lockerbie issue had been resolved, it would also need to address the subject of WMD before Libya would be fully re-integrated into the international community and the American embargo brought to an end. The Clinton administration communicated this message in negotiations with the Libyans in 1999 well before the terrorist attacks of 11 September 2001. Moreover, the Bush administration later sent the same message when it re-opened talks with Tripoli. Consequently, the Iraq War in 2003 and the interception of nuclear technology en route to Libya later that year were not principal driving factors of the decision to forego WMD. Nevertheless, both appeared to increase the pressure on the Gadhafi regime and in doing so may have cemented the decision that had already been taken on WMD, and possibly accelerated the process. In contrast, it is evident that quiet diplomacy and secret negotiations facilitated by the Blair government, and British intelligence officers and diplomats in particular, were pivotal to achieving progress on the issue of Libya's WMD from 1999 to 2003.

CHAPTER FOUR

Dismantlement

Once the decision to forego the pursuit of nuclear weapons was made public on 19 December 2003, the focus shifted to dismantling, removing and destroying key elements of the various programmes. In the nuclear field, the process was notable for its cooperative nature and Libya's desire to involve the IAEA so that the international community could verify the proceedings. The process involved a 'phased' approach to dismantlement which was eventually, although not initially, linked to the incremental provision of rewards by the United States, including the gradual removal of restrictions and sanctions on Libya.

Once Libya's nuclear programme had been dismantled several issues remained for the US and UK, including understanding the full extent of Libya's procurement network so that this type of activity could be more effectively countered in the future. Another task included redirecting Libya's nuclear scientists and technicians to avoid them being enticed to work on weapons programmes in other countries. The Libyan, British and American governments established a Trilateral Steering and Cooperation Committee to address such issues and to facilitate the continued implementation of Tripoli's commitments.

Cooperation not confrontation

During the dismantlement process an emphasis was placed on assisting Libya to implement its decision and on not punishing the Gadhafi regime for its past WMD activities, at the same time as verifying the authenticity of its commitment to disarm. The terminology used was instructive, with references made to 'verification' rather than 'inspections'. The cooperative approach created a permissive environment for dismantling the weapons programmes, with the Libyans usually providing easy access to relevant personnel and facilities. This situation contrasted starkly to the UN Special Commission (UNSCOM) model under which inspections had been imposed on Iraq as a means to verify its disarmament obligations laid out by the Security Council. The Libyan exercise was much more akin to the 'trust and verify' approach to disarmament characteristic of US–Russian arms control initiatives.

The dismantlement process was described by Mahley as 'not a punitive expedition': it did not involve 'dragging things away from a protesting Libyan government'. He stressed the importance of the decision being communicated effectively down the Libyan government hierarchy, which resulted in unrestricted access to all locations, buildings and equipment for the joint US–UK verification teams. According to Mahley, 'in the overwhelming majority of cases' access was granted quickly and 'with outstanding effort on the part of our Libyan hosts'.[1] In large part, this cooperative approach indicated the lack of preconditions imposed by the Libyans at the outset, with no deals sought other than what has been described as a 'mutual commitment to act in good faith'.[2] The Bush administration's claim that its tough approach to countering proliferation – including the 'demonstration effect' of the Iraq War – was responsible for Libya's decision to disarm appears to have unnecessarily tested this good faith, given the Gadhafi regime's sensitivities about not being seen to have given in to American pressure.

International verification

Another notable aspect of the dismantlement process was Libya's desire rapidly to involve the international community, specifically the IAEA and the OPCW, in the nuclear and chemical fields respectively.[3] While the Gadhafi regime evidently wanted to re-establish relations with the United States, it remained highly sensitive about the need to be seen, at home and in the wider Arab world, as having taken the decision of its own free will and not in response to coercion. Moreover, the regime certainly viewed dealing with such organisations as an integral part of Libya's re-entry into the international fold.

The day after the decision became public a Libyan team, led by Matooq, met with ElBaradei in Vienna. The Libyans asked the agency to ensure, through a process of verification, that all of its nuclear activities in future would be under the Safeguards Agreement and for purely peaceful purposes. It was also agreed that Libya would initiate steps to adopt an Additional Protocol to give the IAEA wider inspection rights.[4] Previously, the agency could only visit the TNRC and this contributed in part to its inability to detect Libya's clandestine weapons programme, which was located at other sites removed from the TNRC. Libya subsequently signed an Additional Protocol in March 2004.[5] In further demonstrations of its new non-proliferation credentials, Libya deposited its instrument of ratification of the Comprehensive Test Ban Treaty in January 2004,[6] thereby providing formal evidence of its consent to be bound by the treaty, and also acceded to the CWC.[7] Following its accession to the CWC, the OPCW became responsible for verifying the destruction of Libya's chemical weapons and related materials.

The involvement of the IAEA was not without complications. The agency had been stung by the nuclear revelations that came out of Libya as they demonstrated the wholesale failure of the agency's safeguards. Moreover, the IAEA did not like being kept 'out of the loop' on the secret negotiations prior to 19 December. However, given that the negotiations remained a closely guarded secret within all three governments, it is understandable that the IAEA was not informed, particularly as London and Washington could be not totally confident that Libya would follow through on the WMD decision until it was announced publicly. Nevertheless, a disagreement quickly developed between the agency on one hand, and the Bush administration on the other, regarding the nature and scale of IAEA involvement in the dismantlement process; specifically this focused on who would lead the dismantlement effort and the extent to which the IAEA would be involved in verification. The dispute was fuelled by the agency's very public assessment of Libya's nuclear weapons programme as being only in its initial stages, which contradicted the administration's claim that the Gadhafi regime was much further advanced in terms of fulfilling its weapon ambitions.[8]

The view of the Bush administration was that the lead in verification should be taken by American and British officials because Libya's decision to forego the pursuit of nuclear weapons was the product of the US–UK deal with the Gadhafi regime. For its part, the agency was insistent that the nuclear equipment and materials in Libya constituted part of its 'evidence base' and must 'remain under agency seal and legal custody' until it could 'verify the correctness and completeness of Libya's declarations'.[9] The Gadhafi regime's insistence that the IAEA play a lead role in the verification process served the agency's cause. Without this evidence and access to facilities, the IAEA would not have been able to acquire a complete under-standing of, and therefore to learn from, Libya's Safeguards Agreement violations and the role played by the A.Q. Khan network. In February 2004, for example, ElBaradei noted after talks with Libyan officials that they had been helpful in supplying information on the country's clandes-tine procurement activities.[10]

The disagreement was eventually resolved at a meeting in Vienna on 19 January 2004 involving ElBaradei and senior officials from the United States and Britain, with the latter playing a mediatory role. An agreement was reached under which the IAEA was responsible for verifying that the programme was dismantled correctly, while the United States and Britain were responsible for physically dismantling, removing and destroying the nuclear capabilities. Arrangements were made for IAEA officials to visit Libya separately, although their verification work did involve working alongside joint US–UK teams in certain circumstances, including when items were being catalogued, packed and taken out of the country.[11] The work of the IAEA revolved around several core issues: imports of yellow-cake and other uranium compounds; uranium conversion experiments and procurement plans for the uranium conversion facility; the gas-centrifuge programme; the irradiation of uranium targets; plutonium separation; weapon designs; and the role of the A.Q. Khan network.[12]

Phased disarmament and incremental engagement

In January 2004 representatives from the Libyan, American and British governments agreed to a set of priorities and work-plans for carrying out the dismantlement and verification work in the nuclear, chemical and missile fields. The three-phase approach adopted was dictated prima-rily by logistical constraints and it paved the way for joint US–UK expert groups to visit sites in Libya, to talk to relevant officials, to generate an understanding of the weapons programmes and to determine how to approach dismantlement.[13] One major logistical problem for the United States was its initial lack of a diplomatic platform in Libya. This made the British Embassy pivotal to the dismantlement effort in terms of logistics and broader facilitation. Moreover, American passports could not initially be used for travel to Libya and it took some time before they could be endorsed and the airlines alerted to the changes. These issues were partly symptomatic of the fact that the WMD negotiations were conducted so secretly with only a small handful of American officials involved prior to 19 December 2003, the point at which the full force of the Washington bureaucracy began to assist in the realisation of the Libyan decision.

In response to the completion of each phase, the Bush administration took steps to improve relations with Libya, including the removal of restrictions and the lifting of sanctions. While the dismantlement process and progress on the diplomatic front were not deliberately linked from the outset, the two strands did become aligned as the work moved forward. Indeed, the Bureau for Near East Affairs in the State Department began to look for disarmament milestones as a means of advancing engagement by incrementally 'rewarding' Tripoli. This step-by-step process of engagement in response to progress on WMD was established despite the opposition of some officials within the administration who advocated 'not rewarding bad behaviour',[14] despite the unilateral nature of Libya's decision and the Gadhafi regime's evident commitment to following through.

Phase I

The focus of Phase I was on removing the most proliferation-sensitive materials and equipment, including designs for nuclear weapons, UF_6, L-2 centrifuges and the related equipment and documentation, conversion modules and guidance sets from the North Korean-supplied *Scud*-C missiles. By late January, all of this material had been flown out of Libya for secure storage at the Oak Ridge National Laboratory in the United States.[15]

With respect to international verification, two IAEA officials from nuclear-weapon states had placed the weapon designs under agency seal before their removal. The IAEA also joined US–UK teams as they catalogued, packed and removed nuclear-related items from Libya, placing seals on some centrifuge equipment and documentation for separate storage in the United States.[16]

In terms of American engagement, the Bush administration lifted travel restrictions to Libya in February 2004, allowed travel-related expenditures by US government officials in Libya and permitted firms with pre-sanctions holdings to negotiate contracts for re-entry.[17] The administration also opened an Interests Section in Tripoli and invited the Libyans to do the same in Washington.[18] A delegation including Representatives Tom Lantos and Curt Weldon visited Libya in January 2004, thereby demonstrating Congressional interest in pressing ahead with the engagement process. Weldon visited again in March and Senator Joe Biden also travelled to Libya in the same month.[19] Congressional involvement marked an important turning point, as Congress had initiated the ILSA in the mid-1990s to increase the economic and political pressure on Libya.[20]

Phase II

Phase II began in mid-February 2004 and focused on dismantling and removing the residual elements of the programme, which constituted a far greater proportion of the nuclear equipment compared to the items and materials removed in Phase I. As a result, the logistical challenge increased, with some 1,000 tonnes of equipment removed during this period.[21] Phase II involved continued work on dismantling the centrifuge programme and a contract was signed among Libya, the IAEA and Russia under which 16kg of HEU in fuel assemblies for the IRT-1 research reactor was shipped from the TNRC for blending down into LEU in Russia. The cost of this shipment was covered by the US Department of Energy under the Tripartite Initiative, a cooperative programme involving the United States, Russia and the IAEA to address proliferation and safety concerns by returning to Russia spent and fresh nuclear fuel from Russian-designed reactors located overseas. The United States and the United Kingdom also began paying attention to the redirection of Libya's former WMD personnel.[22]

The Bush administration's engagement with Libya continued apace. In late April 2004, Washington removed most sanctions under the ILSA, although Libya continued to be designated a state sponsor of terrorism by the US State Department, which meant that certain assets of the regime remained frozen and military exports continued to be banned.[23] After Phase II the United States also issued a general licence for trade and investment in Libya.[24] Washington formally resumed direct diplomatic relations in late June 2004 by establishing a Liaison Office in Tripoli.[25]

For its part the British government rewarded Libya with a visit to Tripoli by Blair to meet Gadhafi in late March 2004. This was the first visit by a UK prime minister since King Idris had been toppled from power in 1969.[26] European Commission President Romano Prodi announced in late April that Libya would be asked to join the Barcelona Process as the sole remaining Mediterranean country not yet involved.[27]

Phase III

Phase III was primarily a verification stage and entailed interviewing personnel who had worked on the nuclear and other weapons programmes, including procurement activities, to gain a fuller understanding of their scale. The verification work was 'essentially done' by late September 2004.[28]

In terms of American engagement, President Bush authorised the US Export–Import Bank to support American exports to Libya on 10 September 2004, following assurances from Tripoli that the regime would not acquire or develop nuclear weapons or help other countries to do so.[29] In May 2004,

Libya had announced that its abandonment of WMD included a commitment to cease military dealings with states that it considered to be causes of proliferation concern.[30] While the Libyans did not publicly identify the states covered under this commitment, they were thought to include North Korea, Iran and Syria, although there was no mention of Pakistan.[31] On 20 September 2004, the Bush administration terminated the National Emergency with Respect to Libya that had been imposed in 1986. The executive order removed the remaining economic restrictions on aviation services, allowed a direct scheduled air service and regular charter flights and unblocked approximately US$1.3bn in assets belonging to both Libyan and non-Libyan organisations that had been frozen under US sanctions. However, Libya continued to remain designated a state sponsor of terrorism and this has remained a neuralgic issue in US–Libyan relations.[32] On 24 September 2004, Powell met with Shalgam at the United Nations in New York in the 'first such meeting between top officials of the two countries for more than a quarter century'. In welcoming the completion of Phase III, Powell said the administration wanted to follow the same methodical, step-by-step approach with Libya on terrorism and human rights.[33]

To reward Libya for fulfilling its pledge to abandon WMD completely, EU foreign ministers brought a formal end to 12 years of sanctions in October 2004. This included easing the EU arms embargo. Italy was particularly interested in loosening constraints on Libya, in order to gain its cooperation in stemming illegal immigration into southern Europe from Africa.[34] Beyond the progress on WMD, Tripoli's agreement in August 2004 to pay US$35m to compensate victims of the 1986 Berlin nightclub bombing also helped to contribute to the process of full re-engagement with the EU.

Continuing work

The Trilateral Steering and Cooperation Committee was established to deal with unresolved issues and to monitor Libya's WMD commitments.[35] The committee serves as a forum for experts from the US, UK and Libya to maintain a continuing and confidential dialogue on WMD issues without having to go through international organisations. The 'cooperation' element of the committee's title was evidently deemed to be the most important by the Gadhafi regime, which insisted on its inclusion. This probably reflected a desire to maintain some of its dialogue with the United States and Britain as an equal partner, at least on paper. Under the committee's auspices, groups were set up to deal with outstanding issues in the chemical, missile and nuclear fields. While nuclear issues were largely resolved by the autumn of 2004, one outstanding concern involved the conversion of the IRT-1 reactor to LEU fuel.[36] In late December 2005, Russia's Atomic Energy Agency stated that 14kg of LEU had been sent back to the TNRC under the 2004 agreement.[37]

Another continuing priority for the American and British governments, as well as the IAEA, has been to learn as much as possible about the procurement network that supplied the Libyan nuclear programme so that such transnational supplier operations might be more effectively countered. Some of the material ordered by the Gadhafi regime via the A.Q. Khan network, including centrifuge parts, does not appear to have been delivered to Libya. This has raised concerns that the materials could have been returned to the original supplier or that an unknown third party may have acquired them.[38] For example, one report has referred to 'evidence uncovered by a British–US team of nuclear inspectors' working in Libya confirming 'an exchange of nuclear and missile technology' between Libya and Egypt in late 2003.[39] Completely closing the door on such issues will prove difficult, given the highly secretive and dispersed nature of the A.Q. Khan network's operations. Identifying all the individuals and workshops involved in the network across Europe, Africa and Asia may not prove feasible.

A further priority since early 2004, despite the relative dearth of local nuclear specialists in Libya, has been to avoid the proliferation of human capital to clandestine weapons programmes in other countries. Seeking to avoid 'brain-drain' has involved exploring options for redirecting scientists and technicians towards peaceful employment. It has also meant dealing with demoralised personnel whose careers and professional ambitions have effectively been cut short by the decision to forego WMD. The focus has been on finding for such personnel 'self-gratifying and constructive employment in Libya'.[40] For its part, the regime has been keen to keep personnel employed in the civil nuclear sector on various projects, potentially even including a desalination capability run by a power reactor.

In February 2004, President Bush announced that his administration intended to contribute to the retraining and redirection of Libya's former WMD-related scientists.[41] In doing so, Libya was cited as an example of how the Bush administration wanted to expand 'scientist redirection' efforts beyond the former Soviet Union under its Cooperative Threat Reduction programme.[42] Straw also stated in February 2004 that the United Kingdom had offered to help with a programme to employ former weapons scientists in Libya. Interestingly, in the same statement, Straw indicated a British preference for the geographical coverage of the G-8 Global Partnership against the spread of WMD to become truly global in scope.[43]

Both the United States and Britain have since sent experts to Libya to assist with the redirection of WMD personnel.[44] In October and December 2004, the US State Department led the organisation of workshops involving American and British experts and their Libyan counterparts, focusing on potential collaboration in fields such as medical radioisotope production. One American initiative involves personnel exchanges 'to foster scientific and commercial cooperation between Western and Libyan scientists', and another involves a formal link between the Lawrence Livermore National Laboratory in California and the TNRC.[45]

Conclusion

Dismantling Libya's nuclear infrastructure proved to be a relatively straight-forward exercise because the Gadhafi regime had taken a unilateral and strategic decision to give up its pursuit of nuclear weapons. This paved the way for a cooperative and non-confrontational dismantlement effort much more akin to the 'trust and verify' approach seen in US–Russian arms control than the confrontational UNSCOM model which witnessed the imposition of inspections on Iraq. While the three-phase process was dictated primarily by the logistical challenges associated with the removal of large volumes of equipment and materials, the Bush administration's incremental provision of rewards to Libya in response to the passage of key milestones further smoothed the dismantlement effort, despite the fact that this linkage was not deliberately established at the start and that there was some initial opposition within the administration to 'rewarding' Libya at all.

While the initial sidelining of the IAEA caused some problems in planning the dismantlement process, the agency's verification role was essential to convince the wider international community that Libya had fulfilled its commitment to forego the pursuit of nuclear weapons. The participation of the IAEA was also important as it gave the agency an opportunity to investigate, and therefore to learn from, Libya's Safeguards Agreement violations. Moreover, its involvement was viewed in Tripoli as an integral part of Libya's re-entry into the international community.

CONCLUSION

After seeking to acquire nuclear weapons for over 30 years the Gadhafi regime decided to give up its ambitions in this field in the belief that its core interests were best served by doing so. Libya's economic and security picture had changed dramatically over the preceding decade and the pursuit of nuclear weapons and other WMD had come to be viewed by the regime as a strategic liability, as opposed to a potential deterrent.

Although the Libyan case is highly context specific there has nevertheless been speculation about whether it constitutes a 'model' for addressing the challenges posed by other proliferators. Indeed, Gadhafi himself has called on countries with nuclear and other WMD development programmes to abandon them by stating that 'Libya has become an example to be followed'.[1]

The Libyan case certainly provides a contemporary example of the physical dimensions of a strategic decision to give up the pursuit of nuclear weapons. The provision of unhindered access to any and all facilities as required by inspectors, and in-depth information on past nuclear activities and plans, has ensured the transparency of Libya's nuclear sector to external observers. In the process, this transparency has cemented international confidence in the country's newly peaceful intentions. This experience is also informative in gauging the strategic intent of a country like Iran which has consistently failed to be transparent in its nuclear activities, despite the widespread suspicion that it harbours military objectives and Tehran's claims that its nuclear programme is purely peaceful in nature.

The Libyan case demonstrates that by means of a combination of targeted sanctions, political and diplomatic isolation, export controls and intelligence sharing on nuclear-related shipments and activities, the international community can make the acquisition of nuclear weapons prohibitively costly, in economic and political terms, and in the right context can prompt a unilateral decision to relinquish the pursuit of such weapons. However, as the Libyan example attests, the prevailing political-strategic context is crucial to the efficacy of such measures. Replicating this in a non-Libyan environment is likely to prove very difficult, if not impossible.

The Libya experience highlights the value of applying both carrots and sticks to persuade proliferators to forego the possession or pursuit of nuclear weapons. In this respect, Libya highlights the importance of communicating to proliferators not only the penalties associated with not giving up the pursuit or possession of such weapons, but also the advantages of doing so. This case also demonstrates the importance of quietly communicating and discussing such incentives with proliferators through back-channels and secret negotiations.

There do appear to be parallels between the Libyan and North Korean cases in that both countries' political systems are dominated by a single personality. This is not the case in Iran, where the system is relatively pluralistic. Both the Libyan and North Korean regimes are dominated by leaders in total control of their country's affairs, with the ability to deliver on their pronouncements because of their all-powerful influence on decision-making and implementation. Moreover, both countries have had poor relations with the United States for many years, dominated by their perceptions of vulnerability and insecurity. Hence, if Kim Jong Il opted to take a unilateral and strategic decision to abandon North Korea's nuclear-weapon programme, in return for a series of incremental rewards – including security guarantees from the United States, and potentially from other countries, notably China, similar to those afforded to Gadhafi – he would almost certainly be in a position to deliver. However, the North Korean leader would first need to be convinced – as Gadhafi was between 1999 and 2003 – that his best interests are no longer served by possessing WMD.

The Libyan case also demonstrates that acquiring fissile material remains by far the biggest challenge in developing nuclear weapons. This is particularly the case where countries have failed to establish a technical and scientific infrastructure to support activities necessary for producing weapons-grade uranium or plutonium. Even if an illicit supplier network is available to cut some of the technical corners by providing equipment and start-up materials, the challenge largely remains the same. Conversely, where a country has succeeded in developing a more advanced industrial infrastructure and the associated local expertise, as in the case of Iran, technological infusions from illicit procurement networks are likely to have a much greater impact in advancing weapon ambitions.

Revelations about the A.Q. Khan network's activities vis-à-vis Libya have also generated significant concerns about the true nature and scale of the nuclear black market. The apparent shortcomings of the current non-proliferation regime with regard to deterring and thwarting illicit nuclear activities have also been placed into sharp relief. In large part, concerns about the non-proliferation regime's effectiveness derive from its traditional focus on controlling the nuclear-related activities of state actors and government-to-government transfers. The A.Q. Khan network operated on a transnational basis and was characterised by a complex and interconnected system involving both state and non-state actors operating on a global scale across numerous national boundaries. It remains to be seen whether the A.Q. Khan experience is indicative of the future of nuclear proliferation.

NOTES

Introduction

[1] 'Libyan WMD: Tripoli's statement in full', BBC News Online, 20 December 2003: http://news.bbc.co.uk/2/hi/africa/3336139. stm. Libya possessed more than 3,300 aerial bombs designed for dispersing chemical warfare agent. These bombs were 'irreversibly destroyed' in late February and early March 2004 in a process verified by the OPCW. On 5 March 2004, Libya provided the OPCW with a declaration stating that 23 tonnes of mustard gas had been produced in a chemical weapons facility at Rabta. The Libyans also declared the existence of two chemical-related storage facilities and the presence of 2.9m pounds of precursor materials that could potentially have been used in the manufacture of Sarin nerve agent. Libya has until April 2007 to destroy its 23 tonnes of mustard gas and the US government is currently assessing whether to provide material and financial assistance in the destruction process: 'Libya Completes the First Phase of Chemical Weapons Destruction', Press Release, OPCW, The Hague, 4 March 2004: http://www.opcw. org/html/global/press_releases/2k4/PR7_ 2004.html; 'Libya Timeline: Key events in the lead up to and the aftermath of the Iraq war', *Iraq Watch*, http://www.iraqwatch. org/roundtables/RT4/Libya-Timeline.htm; 'US may help destroy Libya weapons', BBC News Online, 31 March 2006, http:// news.bbc.co.uk/2/hi/africa/4863872.stm. Despite widespread suspicion prior to December 2003 that Libya had an active biological weapons programme, British and American inspectors only found 'a limited research and development' project in the biological area; 'Libya Profile: Biological Overview', Nuclear Threat Initiative Database: http://www.nti.org/e_research/ profiles/Libya/3941.html. In the missile field, Libya agreed to limit its existing capability to systems with a range of 300km or less and a payload capability of no more 500kg in line with the Missile Technology Control Regime (MTCR), an informal suppliers group which coordinates controls on the export of ballistic and cruise missiles and associated technology. This entailed the handing over for removal to the United States of five 800km range *Scud*-C missiles, produced with North Korean assistance, and Libya's agreement to eliminate its much larger inventory of Soviet-supplied *Scud*-B systems estimated at around 80 launchers and up to 240 missiles. 'Libya Timeline', *Iraq Watch*; Carol Giacomo, 'Libya may be allowed to keep some Scud missiles', *Reuters*, 9 March 2004.

[2] The approach was reportedly made by Major Abdel Salam Jalloud, the then deputy chairman of the Revolutionary Command Council of Libya. Jalloud also reportedly approached Egypt's President Nasser for help in acquiring a weapon from China in 1970 and Libya may have wanted a tactical nuclear capability. See

John Wright, *Libya: A Modern History* (London: Croom Helm, 1983), p. 204; John K. Cooley, *Libyan Sandstorm: the Complete Account of Qaddafi's Revolution* (London: Sidgwick & Jackson, 1983), pp. 229–39; Lewis A. Dunn, *Controlling the Bomb: Nuclear Proliferation in the 1980s* (New Haven, CT: Yale University Press, 1982), pp. 14–15, 30–31, 50–51; Mohamed Heikal, *The Road to Ramadan* (London: Collins, 1975), pp. 76–7; Anthony Cordesman, *Weapons of Mass Destruction in the Middle East* (London: Brassey's UK, 1991), pp. 151–3.

3   Shyam Bhatia, *Nuclear Rivals in the Middle East* (London: Routledge, 1988), p. 67.

4   Clyde R. Mark, Congressional Research Service, 'CRS Issue Brief for Congress: Libya' (Washington DC:, The Library of Congress, May 2002), p. 4.

5   Shai Feldman, *Nuclear Weapons and Arms Control in the Middle East* (Cambridge, MA: MIT Press, 1997), pp. 63–5.

6   In 1976 the regime reportedly placed US$1m in gold into a Swiss bank account. The deposit was designed to be a payment for anyone who could supply Tripoli with a nuclear weapon. Another story involved Libya's reported attempt to secure fissionable material from a former CIA officer who reportedly told the Gadhafi regime that he had access to nuclear weapons on the black market and offered to sell them, his offer turned out to be a scam. See Bhatia, *Nuclear Rivals in the Middle East*, pp. 64–71; Leonard S. Spector and Jacqueline R. Smith, *Nuclear Ambitions: The Spread of Nuclear Weapons 1989–1990* (Boulder, CO: Westview, 1990), pp. 175–85.

Chapter One

1   Shahram Chubin, 'Middle East', in Mitchell Reiss and Robert S. Litwak, eds, *Nuclear Proliferation After the Cold War* (Washington DC: Woodrow Wilson Centre Press, 1994), pp. 53–5.

2   Mark, 'CRS Issue Brief for Congress: Libya', pp. 5–7, 12–14.

3   Jon B. Alterman and J. Stephen Morrison, Middle East Note–Africa Notes: Is it Time to Engage Libya? A Conference Report, (Washington DC: Center for Security and International Studies, December 2003), pp. 1-4: http://www.csis.org/media/csis/pubs/anotes_0312.pdf.

4   'Libya', *Country Profiles*, UK Foreign and Commonwealth Office: http://www.fco.gov.uk/servlet/Front?pagename=OpenMarket/Xcelerate/ShowPage&c=Page&cid=1007029394365&a=KCountryProfile&aid=1019149793547.

5   Oye Ogunbadejo, 'Qaddafi's North African Design', *International Security*, vol. 8, no. 1, Summer 1983, p. 155.

6   Milton Viorst, 'The Colonel in His Labyrinth', *Foreign Affairs*, vol. 78, no. 2, March/April 1999, p. 64.

7   Ogunbadejo, 'Qaddafi's North African Design', p. 157.

8   Ronald Bruce St John, 'The Soviet Penetration of Libya', *The World Today*, vol. 38, no. 4, April 1982, pp. 133, 138.

9   'Libya', *The World Factbook*, US Central Intelligence Agency: http://www.cia.gov/cia/publications/factbook/geos/ly.html; Ogunbadejo, 'Qaddafi's North African Design', p. 155; 'Libya', *Country Profiles*, UK Foreign and Commonwealth Office.

10 Office of the Secretary of Defense, *Proliferation: Threat and Response* (Washington DC: Department of Defense, January 2001), pp. 45–9: http://www.defenselink.mil/pubs/ptr20010110.pdf.

11 Joseph Cirincione with Jon B. Wolfstahl and Miriam Rajkimar, *Deadly Arsenals: Tracking Weapons of Mass Destruction* (Washington DC: Carnegie Endowment for International Peace, 2002), pp. 305–12.

12 St John, 'The Soviet Penetration of Libya', p. 133.

13 'Libya: A Country Study', *The Library of Congress Country Studies*, http://countrystudies.us/libya/82.htm.

14 Ogunbadejo, 'Qaddafi's North African Design', p. 156; Viorst, 'The Colonel in His Labyrinth', p. 64.

15 Bhatia, *Nuclear Rivals in the Middle East*, pp. 64–71.

16 Jacob Abadi, 'Pragmatism and Rhetoric in Libya's Policy Toward Israel', *The Journal of Conflict Studies*, vol. 20, no. 1, Fall 2000, pp. 92–3.

17 Ogunbadejo, 'Qaddafi's North African Design', p. 156.

18 Alterman and Morrison, 'Is it Time to Engage Libya?', pp. 1–4.

19 Abadi, 'Pragmatism and Rhetoric in Libya's Policy Toward Israel', pp. 80, 86–7, 97.

20 Roger F. Pajak, 'Soviet Arms Aid to Libya', *Military Review*, July 1976, p. 83.

21 Abadi, 'Pragmatism and Rhetoric in Libya's Policy Toward Israel', p. 87.

22 *Ibid.*, p. 85.

23 Kenneth Katzman, Congressional Research Service, CRS Report for Congress, 'Terrorism: Near Eastern Groups and State Sponsors' (Washington DC: Library of Congress, 13 February 2002): http://www. fas.org/irp/crs/RL31119.pdf.

24 National Foreign Assessment Center, *Patterns of International Terrorism 1980* (Washington, DC: Central Intelligence Agency, June 1981), p. 9, cited in Claudia Wright, 'Libya and the West: Headlong into Confrontation?', *International Affairs*, vol. 58, no. 1, Winter 1981–82, p. 17.

25 Abadi, 'Pragmatism and Rhetoric in Libya's Policy Toward Israel', p. 88.

26 Mark, 'CRS Issue Brief for Congress: Libya', pp. 1, 5–7.

27 George Joffé, 'Libya and Europe', *The Journal of North African Studies*, vol. 6, no. 4, Winter 2001, p. 84.

28 Claudia Wright, 'Libya and the West', p. 23.

29 St John, 'Libyan Foreign Policy: Newfound Flexibility', *Orbis*, vol. 47, no. 3, Summer 2003, p. 472.

30 Andrew J. Pierre, *The Global Politics of Arms Sales* (Princeton, NJ: Princeton University Press, 1982), p. 74.

31 St John, 'The Soviet Penetration of Libya', p. 135.

32 St John, 'Libyan Foreign Policy', p. 472.

33 St John, 'The Soviet Penetration of Libya', p. 136.

34 *Ibid.*, p. 134.

35 Youssef M. Ibrahim, 'Libya and the World: Interview with Colonel Qaddafi, 10 December 1979', *Survival*, vol. 22, no. 2, March/April 1980, pp. 80–82.

36 Claudia Wright, 'Libya and the West', p. 38.

37 Tim Zimmermann, 'The American Bombing of Libya: A success for coercive diplomacy?', *Survival*, vol. 29, no. 3, May/June 1987, pp. 196–9.

38 Ambassador Ronald Neumann, Deputy Assistant Secretary of State for Near Eastern Affairs, Testimony before the Senate Foreign Relations Subcommittee for Near Eastern and South Asian Affairs, 4 May 2000. See: 'Neumann's Senate Testimony on US Policy Toward Libya', 4 May 2000: http://www. globalsecurity.org/wmd/library/news/ libya/000504-libya-usia1.htm.

39 National Foreign Assessment Center, *Patterns of International Terrorism 1980*, (Washington DC: US Central Intelligence Agency, June 1981), p. 9, cited in Claudia Wright, 'Libya and the West', p. 17.

40 St John, 'Libyan Foreign Policy', pp. 463–4.

41 'Neumann's Senate Testimony on US Policy Toward Libya', 4 May 2000.

42 Tim Zimmermann, 'The American Bombing of Libya', pp. 196–9.

43 Mark, 'CRS Issue Brief for Congress: Libya', pp. 5–7.

44 National Security Decision Directive 205, *Acting Against Libyan Support for International Terrorism* (Washington DC: The White House, 8 January 1986): http:// www.gwu.edu/~nsarchiv/NSAEBB/ NSAEBB55/nsdd205.pdf.

45 Mark, 'CRS Issue Brief for Congress: Libya', pp. 5–7.

46 *Ibid.*, pp. 5–7.

47 'Neumann's Senate Testimony on US Policy Toward Libya', 4 May 2000.

48 Frederick Zilian, Jr, 'The US Raid on Libya – and NATO', *Orbis*, no. 30, Fall 1986, pp. 499, 509–10.

49 Britain had officially broken off diplomatic relations with Libya in 1984 after the shooting of WPC Yvonne Fletcher

in St James's Square outside the Libyan Embassy.

50 'Libya', *Country Profiles,* UK Foreign and Commonwealth Office.

51 'Libya: IRT-1', Research Reactor Database, International Atomic Energy Agency, http://www.iaea.org/worldatom/rrdb/; 'Documentation: NPT Parties', *PPNN Newsbrief,* no. 24, Fourth Quarter 1993, p. 23: http://www.ppnn.soton.ac.uk/nb24. pdf; Bhatia, *Nuclear Rivals in the Middle East,* p. 68.

52 INFCIRC/282: The Text of the Agreement of 8 July 1980 Between the Libyan Arab Jamahiriya and the Agency for the Application of Safeguards in Connection with the Treaty on the Non-Proliferation of Nuclear Weapons (Vienna: International Atomic Energy Agency, October 1980).

53 Ibrahim, 'Libya and the World', pp. 80–82.

54 'Libya: A Country Study', *The Library of Congress Country Studies,* The Library of Congress: http://lcweb2.loc.gov/frd/cs/lytoc.html.

55 Craig R. Black, *Deterring Libya: The Strategic Culture of Muammar Qaddafi,* The Counterproliferation Papers: Future Warfare Series No. 8 (Maxwell Air Force Base, AL: USAF Counterproliferation Center, October 2000), p. 6: http://www.au.af.mil/au/awc/awcgate/cpc-pubs/black.pdf.

56 Spector and Smith, *Nuclear Ambitions,* p. 178. See also Frank Barnaby, *The Invisible Bomb: The Nuclear Arms Race in the Middle East* (London: I.B. Tauris, 1989), p. 150; Black, *Deterring Libya,* p. 6.

57 Greg Giles, Candice Cohen, Christy Razzano and Sara Whitaker, *Future Global Nuclear Threats,* a report prepared for the Advanced Systems and Concepts Office (Ft Belvoir, VA: Defense Threat Reduction Agency, 4 June 2001), pp. A27–8.

58 Abadi, 'Pragmatism and Rhetoric in Libya's Policy Toward Israel', p. 91.

59 *Ibid.,* p. 91.

60 *Ibid.,* p. 93.

61 Feldman, *Nuclear Weapons and Arms Control in the Middle East,* pp. 63–5.

62 Abadi, 'Pragmatism and Rhetoric in Libya's Policy Toward Israel', p. 92.

63 Mati Peled, *Ha'aretz* (Hebrew), 9 September 1985, pp. 61–3 (via the Nuclear Threat Initiative [NTI] Nuclear Database, http://www.nti.org/db/nuclear/1986/n8600658.htm).

64 'Beyond the Axis of Evil: Additional Threats from Weapons of Mass Destruction', Address by John R. Bolton, Under Secretary of State for Arms Control and International Security, to the Heritage Foundation, Washington DC, 6 May 2002: http://www.state.gov/t/us/rm/9962.htm.

65 Paul Kerr, 'IAEA praises Libya for disarmament efforts', *Arms Control Today,* April 2004: http://www.armscontrol.org/act/2004_04/Libya.asp.

66 See, for example, Robert Waller, 'Libyan Threat Perception', *Jane's Intelligence Review,* vol. 7, no. 9, September 1995, p. 408; *Future Global Nuclear Threats,* pp. A27–8.

67 Spector and Smith, *Nuclear Ambitions,* p. 183.

68 Director General, IAEA, *Implementation of the NPT Safeguards Agreement of the Socialist People's Libyan Arab Jamahiriya* (Vienna: IAEA, 28 May 2004), pp. 4–5: http://www.fas.org/nuke/guide/libya/iaea0504.pdf; 'Japanese Parts Used in Libya's Nuke Program', *Herald Asahi,* 13 March 2004.

69 Chubin, 'Middle East', p. 53.

70 Spector and Smith, *Nuclear Ambitions,* p. 178.

71 *Nuclear Proliferation News,* 1 June 1995, p. 8, via World Information Service on Energy: Uranium Project, published by WISE News Communiqué, 16 June 1995: http://www.antenna.nl/wise/433-4/brief.html.

Chapter Two

1   Cooley, *Libya Sandstorm*, p. 231.
2   Bhatia, *Nuclear Rivals in the Middle East*, p. 70.
3   See 'Libya: A Country Study', *The Library of Congress Country Studies*; Bhatia, *Nuclear Rivals in the Middle East*, p. 68; 'Annex 8: Nuclear Infrastructures of Argentina and Brazil', *Nuclear Technologies and Non-Proliferation Policies*, Issue 2, 2001: http://npc.sarov.ru/english/digest/digest_2_2001.html; Richard Kessler, 'Peron Widow's Libyan Visit Revives Talk of Nuclear Link', *Nucleonics Week*, 8 September 1988, pp. 6–7.
4   'ANSTO Briefing: Response to Issues Raised', (Lucas Heights, NSW: Australian Nuclear Science and Technology Organisation [ANSTO], 8 June 2000).
5   Libya continued its investigations into exploitable uranium reserves during the 1980s. The IAEA approved two technical cooperation projects with Libya in 1979 and 1980 on prospecting for nuclear raw material deposits, which were completed in September 1982 and October 1987, respectively. Indeed, up to four potential uranium deposits were under active exploration during the mid-1980s although it does not appear that any of them proved to be exploitable. Belgatom, Belgonucleaire, Union Mirac and Brazil's Mineral Resources Prospecting Company reportedly provided technical assistance for the exploration of uranium deposits in Libya during the early to mid-1980s. Project Number LIB/3/003, Nuclear Raw Materials, approved for the first time in 1979, was completed on 28 November 1983. The project involved the National Scientific Research Council; Department of Exploration. See Department of Technical Cooperation, International Atomic Energy Authority: http://www-tc.iaea.org/tcweb/projectinfo/default.asp; Project Number LIB/3/004, Nuclear Raw Materials, first approved 1980, completed 26 October 1987. The project involved the National Scientific Research Council, Department of

Prospecting and Mining. See Department of Technical Cooperation, International Atomic Energy Authority, http://www-tc.iaea.org/tcweb/projectinfo/default.asp; Tripoli Television, 0810 GMT 6 May 1985, in BBC Summary of World Broadcasts, 21 May 1985, Part 4: The Middle East, Africa and Latin America, Weekly Economic Report, ME/W1339/A1/6; Spector, *Going Nuclear: the Spread of Nuclear Weapons, 1986–87* (Cambridge, MA: Ballinger Publishing Company, 1987), p. 157; Spector and Smith, *Nuclear Ambitions*, pp. 175–85; OTA, *Technology Transfer to the Middle East* (Washington DC: US Congress, September 1984), OTA-1 SC-173, p. 380: http://www.wws.princeton.edu/ota/ns20/year_f.html; Sergio Dani, 'Mining Activities with Libya', *Gazeta Mercantil* (São Paulo), 6 November 1984, p. 14, in *FBIS Worldwide Report*, 14 January 1985, p. 41, via NTI Nuclear Database: http://www.nti.org/db/nuclear/1985/n8500212.htm.
6   Bhatia, *Nuclear Rivals in the Middle East*, pp. 65–7.
7   Ann MacLachlan and Mike Knapik, 'Belgium and Libya will Sign an Agreement on Nuclear Cooperation', *Nucleonics Week*, vol. 25, no. 21, 24 May 1984, p. 5. According to Cooley, the White House intervened in addition to the State Department. Cooley, *Libya Sandstorm*, p. 231.
8   *Ibid.*, p. 230.
9   See Bhatia, *Nuclear Rivals in the Middle East*, p. 68; Barnaby, *The Invisible Bomb*, pp. 98–9. On the failed Libyan–French deal, see also Feldman, *Nuclear Weapons and Arms Control in the Middle East*, pp. 63–5; Roger F. Pajak, 'Nuclear status and policies of the Middle East countries', *International Affairs*, vol. 59, no. 4, Autumn 1983, pp. 600–601.
10 'Nuclear Chronology, 1968–1979, Libya', NTI Nuclear Database, http://www.nti.org/e_research/profiles/Libya/4132.html.
11 Ischebeck, 'Pakistan's Nuclear Programme: Policies, Achievements and Potential for

National Development', in Ishebeck and Götz Neuneck, eds, *Cooperative Policies for Preventing and Controlling the Spread of Missiles and Nuclear Weapons: Policies and Perspectives in Southern Asia* (Baden-Baden: Nomos, 1996), p. 67.

12   Cooley, *Libya Sandstorm*, pp. 232–3; OTA, *Technology Transfer to the Middle East*, p. 397; Spector and Smith, *Nuclear Ambitions*, pp. 175–85.

13   Spector and Smith, *Nuclear Ambitions*, p. 176; Ischebeck, 'Pakistan's Nuclear Programme', p. 67.

14   Spector and Smith, *Nuclear Ambitions*, pp. 175–85; Cordesman, *Weapons of Mass Destruction in the Middle East*, p. 152.

15   Gloria Duffy, *Soviet nuclear energy: domestic and international policies* (Santa Monica, CA: RAND, December 1979), pp. 84–5. This work was prepared for the US Department of Energy. See also OTA, *Technology Transfer to the Middle East*, p. 395.

16   MacLachlan, 'Libyans Are Seeking Abroad International Cooperation in Nuclear Area', *Nucleonics Week*, vol. 25, no. 39, 27 September 1984, p. 1.

17   Atomstroyexport comes under MINATOM. 'Atomstroyexport', Russia, NIS Profiles, NTI Nuclear Database:, http://www.nti.org/db/nisprofs/russia/reactor/research/without/atomstro.htm.

18   See ENS Nucnet, 6 February 1992, via 'Russia: Kurchatov Institute (Russian Research Center)', NTI Database: http://www.nti.org/db/nisprofs/russia/reactor/research/with/kurchato.htm . See also R. Adam Moody, 'Armageddon for Hire', *Jane's International Defense Review*, vol. 30, February 1997, p. 21.

19   Claudia Wright, 'Libya and the West', pp. 38–41.

20   See 'Libya: IRT-1', Research Reactor Database, IAEA.

21   Pajak, 'Soviet Arms Aid to Libya' p. 86.

22   Pajak, 'Nuclear status and policies of the Middle East countries', pp. 600–601.

23   Mohamed M. Megahed, 'Nuclear Desalination: History and Prospects', *Desalination*, no. 135, 2001, pp. 169–85:

http://www.desline.com/articoli/4047.pdf. See also Cirincione with Wolfstahl and Rajkimar, *Deadly Arsenals*, p. 311.

24   See Mark, 'CRS Issue Brief for Congress: Libya', p.8; Jonathan Bearman, 'The Conflict in Chad', in *Qadhafi's Libya* (London: Zed Books, 1986), pp. 203–6.

25   'Relations with Chad', 'External Affairs: Libya', *Jane's Sentinel Security Assessments* 9 November 2001: http://sentinel.janes.com/public/sentinel/index.shtml.

26   Director General, IAEA, *Implementation of the NPT Safeguards Agreement*, 28 May 2004, Annex 1, p. 2.

27   *Ibid.*, p. 2.

28   *Ibid.*, p. 2.

29   See for example Cooley, *Libya Sandstorm*, pp. 202–4; Claudia Wright, 'Libya and the West', p. 33; OTA, *Technology Transfer to the Middle East*, p. 386.

30   Cordesman, *Weapons of Mass Destruction in the Middle East*, pp. 151–3; Barnaby, *The Invisible Bomb*, p. 104; 'WMD Around the World: Libya', Federation of American Scientists, http://www.fas.org/nuke/guide/libya/; Spector and Smith, *Nuclear Ambitions*, pp. 175–85; W.P.S. Sidhu, 'Pakistan's Bomb: A Quest for Credibility', *Jane's Intelligence Review*, vol. 8, no. 6, June 1996, p. 278.

31   See Cordesman, *Weapons of Mass Destruction in the Middle East*, pp. 151–3; Cooley, *Libya Sandstorm*, pp. 229–39.

32   Bhatia, *Nuclear Rivals in the Middle East*, pp. 64–71; Spector and Smith, *Nuclear Ambitions*, pp. 175–85; See 'WMD Around the World: Libya', Federation of American Scientists; 'Libya: A Country Study', *The Library of Congress Country Studies*; Cooley, *Libya Sandstorm*, pp. 229–39; Cordesman, *Weapons of Mass Destruction in the Middle East*, pp. 151–3.

33   *Ibid.*

34   Rodney W. Jones, *Nuclear Proliferation: Islam, the Bomb, and South Asia*, Washington Papers, no. 82 (Washington DC: Centre for Strategic and International Studies, 1981), pp. 48–9.

35   Bhatia, *Nuclear Rivals in the Middle East*, pp. 97–8.

36 *Ibid.* pp. 64-71; Ischebeck, 'Pakistan's Nuclear Programme', pp. 85, 78.

37 *Ibid.,* pp. 85, 78.

38 Sidhu, 'Pakistan's Bomb', p. 279.

39 Maj.–Gen. D.K. Palit, *Pakistan's Islamic Bomb* (New Delhi: Vikas Publishing House, 1979), pp. 23–44.

40 See Ischebeck, 'Pakistan's Nuclear Programme', pp. 85, 78; Mycle Schneide, *Politis-Le-Citoyen* (Paris), 22–28 February 1990, pp. 50–55, in *FBIS Nuclear Developments,* 18 July 1990, pp. 26–30, NTI Nuclear Database, http://www.nti.org/db/nuclear/1990/n9004558.htm.

41 Bhatia, *Nuclear Rivals in the Middle East,* pp. 64–71.

42 Cordesman, *Weapons of Mass Destruction in the Middle East,* pp. 151–3; Sidhu, 'Pakistan's Bomb', p. 278.

43 Cooley, *Libya Sandstorm,* p. 232.

44 Jones, *Nuclear Proliferation,* pp. 48–49.

45 See: Bhatia, *Nuclear Rivals in the Middle East,* pp. 64–71; Claudia Wright, 'Libya and the West', p. 41; Cooley, *Libya Sandstorm,* pp. 229–39; Jones, *Nuclear Proliferation,* pp. 48–49.

46 Libya's efforts to build ballistic missiles during the same period contributed to international concerns about the country's nuclear ambitions. The regime's missile efforts, similar to the nuclear arena, were notable because of their reliance on foreign assistance. For example, in 1979 the West German firm OTRAG established operations in Libya and began developing an ostensibly civilian sounding rocket with a reported range of 300–500km in a surface-to-surface mode. Despite its claim to be a commercial space launch entity, OTRAG left in August 1981 under pressure from the West German government. This coincided with Israeli reports that Syria had signed a contract with OTRAG for 300 and 2,000km range ballistic missiles. See: 'Libyans get nuclear missile system', *Guardian,* 21 March 1981; 'Rocket Fired by Libya', *Daily Telegraph,* 7 March 1981; J. Vinocur, 'Launching of Suborbital Rocket in Libya by West Germany', *International Herald Tribune,* 13 March 1981; D. Fairhill, 'Missile Fears Denied', *Guardian,* 1 June 1981; 'West German Rocket Firm Quits Libya', *Daily Telegraph,* 30 December 1981.

47 OTA, *Technology Transfer to the Middle East,* p. 386.

48 A further 48 targets were irradiated in the IRT-1 but were not processed. Director General, IAEA, *Implementation of the NPT Safeguards Agreement,* 20 February 2004, p. 6.

49 'Annex 8: Nuclear Infrastructures of Argentina and Brazil', *Nuclear Technologies and Non-Proliferation Policies,* Issue 2, 2001.

50 According to Henry S. Rowen and Richard Brody, their estimate was based on reactor operations designed for the most efficient generation of electricity. Moreover, they contended that while the resultant 'high burnup plutonium' would contain 'a substantial proportion of the isotope Pu-240', it would still be usable in a nuclear weapon with 1–20 kilotonne yields. It was also noted that weapons-grade plutonium with a higher explosive yield could be produced in power reactors by extracting fuel rods after short periods of irradiation. See Rowen and Brody, 'Nuclear Potential and Possible Contingencies', in Joseph A. Yager, ed., *Nonproliferation and US Foreign Policy* (Washington DC: Brookings, 1980), p. 208.

51 Project Number LIB/9/005, Siting of Nuclear Power Plant, first approved 1983, completed 23 December 1985. The project involved Libya's National Scientific Research Council. See Department of Technical Cooperation, International Atomic Energy Agency: http://www-tc.iaea.org/tcweb/projectinfo/default.asp.

52 Project Number LIB/4/005, Nuclear Power Plant, first approved 1984, cancelled 30 June 1986. The project involved the National Scientific Research Council, Department of Power. See Department of Technical Cooperation, International Atomic Energy Agency: http://www-tc.iaea.org/tcweb/projectinfo/default.asp.

53 'Libya Abandons Plans for First Unit', *Nuclear Engineering International,* April

1986, p. 6; 'Moscow Retreats from Libyan Nuclear Scheme', *MidEast Markets*, 3 August 1987; *Nuclear Engineering International*, December 1987, cited in 'Other Proliferation Developments', *PPNN Newsbrief*, no. 1, March 1988, p. 2: http://www.ppnn.soton.ac.uk/nb01.pdf; K.D. Kapur, *Soviet Nuclear Non-Proliferation Diplomacy and the Third World* (New Delhi: Konark Publishers, 1993), p. 148; 'WMD Around the World: Libya', Federation of American Scientists.

54 'WMD Around the World: Libya', Federation of American Scientists. The same account is given in Barnaby, *The Invisible Bomb*, pp. 98–9; MacLachlan and Knapik, 'Belgium and Libya', p. 5.

55 OTA, *Technology Transfer to the Middle East*, p.380.

56 MacLachlan and Knapik, 'Belgium and Libya', p.5; 'WMD Around the World: Libya', Federation of American Scientists; Spector and Smith, *Nuclear Ambitions*, pp. 175–85. See 'Soviets Draw Back From Helping Libyan Programme', *Nuclear Engineering International*, December 1987, p. 27.

57 'WMD Around the World: Libya', Federation of American Scientists; Barnaby, *The Invisible Bomb*, pp. 98–9.

58 MacLachlan and Knapik, 'Belgium and Libya', p.5.

59 Highly enriched uranium metal can also be prepared using this process for nuclear weapons.

60 Director General, IAEA, *Implementation of the NPT Safeguards Agreement*, 28 May 2004, p. 4.

61 *Ibid.* pp. 4–5; 'Japanese Parts Used in Libya's Nuke Program', *Herald Asahi*, 13 March 2004.

62 For natural uranium-fuelled reactors the U_3O_8 concentrate is basically refined and converted to uranium dioxide. No enrichment of the uranium is necessary.

63 Director General, IAEA, *Implementation of the NPT Safeguards Agreement*, 28 May 2004, pp. 3–4.

64 *Ibid.*, pp. 3–4.

65 *Ibid.*, p. 4.

66 Spector, *Going Nuclear*, p. 157; Spector and Smith, *Nuclear Ambitions*, pp. 175–85; Cordesman, *Weapons of Mass Destruction in the Middle East*, pp. 151–3.

67 Director General, IAEA, *Implementation of the NPT Safeguards Agreement*, 28 May 2004, pp. 3–4.

68 *Ibid.*, pp. 4–5; 'Japanese Parts Used in Libya's Nuke Program', *Herald Asahi*, 13 March 2004.

69 Director General, IAEA, *Implementation of the NPT Safeguards Agreement*, 28 May 2004, Annex 1, p. 5; According to the *Los Angeles Times*, the foreign expert was a German flight engineer. Douglas Frantz and Josh Meyer, 'For Sale: Nuclear Expertise', *Los Angeles Times*, 22 February 2004.

70 Director General, IAEA, *Implementation of the NPT Safeguards Agreement*, 28 May 2004, Annex 1, pp. 5–6.

71 Frantz and Meyer, 'For Sale'.

72 Director General, IAEA, *Implementation of the NPT Safeguards Agreement*, 28 May 2004, Annex 1, pp. 5–6.

73 'Annex 8: Nuclear Infrastructures of Argentina and Brazil', *Nuclear Technologies and Non-Proliferation Policies,* Issue 2, 2001.

74 Nothing significant appears to have occurred during the first part of the 1990s apart from various reports about Libya capitalising on the dissolution of the Soviet Union by seeking to acquire nuclear technology and materials, and to recruit scientists.

75 Interestingly, Tripoli and Moscow commenced talks on renewed nuclear cooperation in January and November 2000, focusing on the refurbishment of the TNRC. See 'Unclassified Report to Congress on the Acquisition of Technology Relating to Weapons of Mass Destruction and Advanced Conventional Munitions: 1 January Through 30 June 2001', http://www.cia.gov/cia/reports/721_reports/jan_jun2001.htm; Statement by Spector, Deputy Director, Center for Nonproliferation Studies, Monterey Institute of International Studies, before the Subcommittee on International Security,

Proliferation and Federal Services of the US Senate Committee on Governmental Affairs, 6 June 2002: http://www.senate.gov/~govt-aff/060602specter.pdf.

76 'Report to the President of the United States', (Washington DC: The Commission on the Intelligence Capabilities of the United States Regarding Weapons of Mass Destruction, , 31 March 2005), p. 257: http://www.wmd.gov/report/.

77 Ambassador Donald Mahley, 'Dismantling Libyan Weapons: Lessons Learned', *The Arena*, no. 10, November 2004, p. 5.

78 Bill Gertz, 'Libyan sincerity on arms in doubt', *Washington Times*, 9 September 2004.

79 Royal Malaysia Police, 'Press Release by Inspector General of Police in Relation to Investigation on the Alleged Production of Components for Libya's Uranium Enrichment Programme', 20 February 2004: http://www.rmp.gov.my/rmp03/040220scomi_eng.htm; Gertz, 'Libyan sincerity on arms in doubt'.

80 Director General, IAEA, *Implementation of the NPT Safeguards Agreement*, 28 May 2004, p. 7.

81 National Board for Scientific Research, Libya: http://www.nasrlibya.net/english.html.

82 See Royal Malaysia Police, 'Press Release by Inspector General of Police'; Gertz, 'Libyan sincerity on arms in doubt'.

83 Interview in *Der Spiegel* quoted by Ian Traynor in 'Nuclear chief tells of black market in bomb equipment', *Guardian*, 26 January 2004, p. 14.

84 Traynor, 'Nuclear chief tells of black market in bomb equipment', p. 14; Anwar Iqbal, 'Khan network supplied N-parts made in Europe, Southeast Asia', *Dawn* (online edition), 14 October 2004, http://www.dawn.com/2004/10/14/top9.htm.

85 'A.Q. Khan & Libya', GlobalSecurity.Org.

86 Stephen Fidler and Mark Huband, 'Turks and South Africans helped Libya's secret nuclear arms project', *Financial Times*, 10 June 2004, p. 11.

87 Iqbal, 'Khan network supplied N-parts made in Europe, Southeast Asia'.

88 Andrew Koch, 'The nuclear network: Khanfessions of a proliferator', *Jane's Defence Weekly*, 24 February 2004.

89 Centrifuges incorporate some 100 or so separate components including, for example, rotors, ring magnets, pipes, valves, baffles and vacuum pumps.

90 Raymond Bonner, 'Did Tenet Exaggerate Malaysian Plant's Demise?', *New York Times*, 9 February 2004, p. 4; Agence France-Presse, 'Libyan nuclear workers trained in Malaysia: official', 29 May 2004, via Channel News Asia, Singapore..

91 Bonner, 'Did Tenet Exaggerate Malaysian Plant's Demise?', p. 4.

92 *Ibid.*, p. 4; Gertz, 'Libyan sincerity on arms in doubt'.

93 Anwar Iqbal, 'Khan network supplied N-parts made in Europe, Southeast Asia'; Fidler and Huband, 'Turks and South Africans helped Libya's secret nuclear arms project', *Financial Times*, 10 June 2004, p. 11.

94 *Ibid.* p. 11; Royal Malaysia Police, 'Press Release by Inspector General of Police'.

95 Illicit trade networks have long exploited the UAE as a key transhipment point for material such as sensitive technologies and drugs. In 2003, electronic and machinery products accounted for 21% of re-exports in the UAE. 'UAE Economic Overview and Guide to Doing Business', UK Trade and Investment: https://www.uktradeinvest.gov.uk.

96 Fidler and Victoria Burnett, 'Connections Across the World Were Involved in Offering Sensitive Technology to at Least Three Countries', *Financial Times*, 7 April 2004.

97 Agence France Presse, 'Libyan nuclear workers trained in Malaysia'.

98 Bonner, 'The Two Faces of Nuclear Suspect in Malaysia', *International Herald Tribune*, 20 February 2004, p. 1.

99 Elizabeth Nash, 'Spanish Firms in Secret Arms Trade to Libya', *Independent*, 12 February 2004.

100 Director General, IAEA, *Implementation of the NPT Safeguards Agreement*, 28 May 2004, Annex 1, p. 6; Fidler and Huband, 'Turks and South Africans helped Libya's secret nuclear arms project', p. 11.

101 David Albright and Corey Hinderstein, 'Libya's Gas Centrifuge Procurement: Much Remains Undiscovered', Institute for Science and Intenational Security, 1 March 2004, http://www.isis-online.org/publications/libya/cent_procure.html; Sammy Salama and Lydia Hansell, 'Companies Reported to Have Sold or Attempted to Sell Libya Gas Centrifuge Components, Issue Brief', NTI Database, March 2005: http://www.nti.org/e_research/e3_60a.html.

102 Director General, IAEA, *Implementation of the NPT Safeguards Agreement*, 20 February 2004, p. 5; Iqbal, 'Khan network supplied N-parts made in Europe, Southeast Asia'.

103 Director General, IAEA, *Implementation of the NPT Safeguards Agreement*, 20 February 2004, p. 5; Iqbal, 'Khan network supplied N-parts made in Europe, Southeast Asia'.

104 Director General, IAEA, *Implementation of the NPT Safeguards Agreement*, 28 May 2004, Annex 1, p. 5.

105 Director General, IAEA, *Implementation of the NPT Safeguards Agreement*, 20 February 2004, p. 5.

106 *Ibid.*, p. 5.

107 Director General, IAEA, *Implementation of the NPT Safeguards Agreement*, 28 May 2004, Annex 1, p. 5.

108 Paul Kerr, 'IAEA: Questions Remain About Libya', *Arms Control Today*, July/August 2004, http://www.armscontrol.org/act/2004_07-08/IAEAandLibya.asp.

109 Director General, IAEA, *Implementation of the NPT Safeguards Agreement*, 28 May 2004, Annex 1, pp. 5–6.

110 Albright, President and Founder, Institute for Science and Security, 'International Smuggling Networks: Weapons of Mass Destruction Counterproliferation Initiatives', statement before the US Senate Committee on Governmental Affairs, 23 June 2004: http://www.senate.gov/~govt-aff/index.cfm?Fuseaction=Hearings.Testimony&HearingID=185&WitnessID=673.

111 Director General, IAEA, *Implementation of the NPT Safeguards Agreement*, 28 May 2004, Annex 1, pp. 5–6.

112 *Ibid.* Annex 1, pp. 5–6.

113 *Ibid.* Annex 1, pp. 5–6.

114 John Lancaster and Kamran Khan, 'Pakistan Confesses to Aiding Nuclear Efforts', *Washington Post*, 2 February 2004.

115 David Sanger and William J. Broad, 'Evidence Is Cited Linking Koreans to Libya Uranium', *New York Times*, 23 May 2004.

116 See for example Seymour Hersh, 'The Deal: Why is Washington going easy on Pakistan's nuclear black marketers?', *The New Yorker*, 8 March 2004.

117 Director General, IAEA, *Implementation of the NPT Safeguards Agreement*, 20 February 2004, pp. 6–7.

118 Joby Warrick and Peter Slevin, 'Probe of Libya Finds Nuclear Black Market', *Washington Post*, 24 January 2004; Broad, Sanger and Bonner, 'A Tale of Nuclear Proliferation: How Pakistani Built His Network', *New York Times*, 12 February 2004, p. A1; Owen Bowcott, John Aglionby and Traynor, 'Atomic Secrets: Businessman Under Scrutiny 25 Years Ago After Ordering Unusual Supplies', *Guardian*, 5 March 2004.

119 Iqbal, 'Khan network supplied N-parts made in Europe, Southeast Asia'.

120 Director General, IAEA, *Implementation of the NPT Safeguards Agreement*, 20 February 2004, pp.6–7.

121 Director General, IAEA, *Implementation of the NPT Safeguards Agreement*, 28 May 2004, pp. 4–5.

122 Director General, IAEA, *Implementation of the NPT Safeguards Agreement*, 20 February 2004, p. 4; Director General, IAEA, *Implementation of the NPT Safeguards Agreement*, 28 May 2004, Annex 1, p. 3.

123 Sanger and Broad, 'Evidence is Cited Linking North Koreans to Libyan Uranium'.

124 Dafna Linzer, 'US Misled Allies About Nuclear Export North Korea Sent Material To Pakistan, Not to Libya', *Washington Post*, 20 March 2005, p. A1.

125 Sanger and Broad, 'Tests Said to Tie Deal on Uranium to North Korea', *New York Times*, 2 February 2005; see also Traynor,

'North Korean nuclear trade exposed', *Guardian*, 24 May 2004, p. 12.

[126] Broad and Sanger, 'Khan was selling a complete package', *International Herald Tribune*, 22 March 2005; Director General, IAEA, *Implementation of the NPT Safeguards Agreement*, 28 May 2004, p. 7.

[127] Andrew Koch, 'The nuclear network'; 'Chinese Warhead Drawings Among Libyan Documents', *Los Angeles Times*, 16 February 2004; Broad and Sanger, 'Khan was selling a complete package'. See also: 'Libya Was Far From Building Nuclear Bomb', *Wall Street Journal*, 23 February 2004; 'Libya nuke prints from China', *Associated Press*, 15 February 2004; Warrick and Slevin, 'Libyan Arms Designs Traced Back to China', *Washington Post*, 15 February 2004, p. A1.

[128] Director General, IAEA, *Implementation of the NPT Safeguards Agreement*, 28 May 2004, p. 3.

[129] Broad and Sanger, 'Warhead Blueprints Link Libya Project To Pakistan Figure', *New York Times*, 3 February 2004; Frantz and Meyer, 'For Sale'.

[130] Director General, IAEA, *Implementation of the NPT Safeguards Agreement*, 28 May 2004, p. 3.

[131] *Ibid.*, p. 7.

[132] Mahley, 'Dismantling Libyan Weapons', p. 2.

[133] Richard Stone, 'Agencies Plan Exchange With Libya's Former Weaponeers', *Science*, vol. 308, no. 5719, 8 April 2005, pp.185–6.

[134] Mahley, 'Dismantling Libyan Weapons', p. 7.

[135] 'Report to the President of the United States', The Commission on the Intelligence Capabilities of the US Regarding WMD, pp. 259–60.

[136] Mahley, 'Dismantling Libyan Weapons', pp. 7–8.

Chapter Three

[1] 'Libyan WMD: Tripoli's statement in full', BBC News Online.

[2] 'Security Council hails Libya's cooperation with UN on weapons verification', UN News Service, 23 December 2003: http://www.globalsecurity.org/wmd/library/news/libya/libya-031223-unnews01.htm.

[3] Gadhafi quoted by John Bolton, 'The NPT: A Crisis of Non-Compliance', Statement to the Third Session of the Preparatory Committee for the 2005 Review Conference of the Treaty on the Non-Proliferation of Nuclear Weapons, New York City, 27 April 2004: http://www.state.gov/t/us/rm/31848.htm.

[4] 'The New Gadhafi', *60 Minutes*, 10 March 2004, CBS News: http://www.cbsnews.com/stories/2004/03/09/60II/main604971.shtml.

[5] Kerr, 'IAEA praises Libya for disarmament efforts'.

[6] Kathleen Knox, 'EU–Libya: Ghaddafi visits Brussels in Tripoli's latest step coming in from the Cold', Radio Free Europe/Radio Liberty, 27 April 2004.

[7] Patrick E. Tyler, 'Blair may meet Qaddafi soon', *International Herald Tribune*, 11 February 2004, p. 3.

[8] 'Libyan WMD: Tripoli's statement in full', BBC News Online; 'Security Council hails Libya's cooperation with UN on weapons verification', UN News Service.

[9] Mary Dejevsky, 'Libya decided 10 years ago against developing WMD without pressure, Foreign Minister says', *Independent*, 11 February 2004, p. 6; Anton La Guardia, 'Blair talks with Gaddafi hinge on WPC progress', *Daily Telegraph*, 11 February 2004, p. 2.

[10] Dejevsky, 'Libya decided 10 years ago against developing WMD without pressure, Foreign Minister says', p. 6; Laurie Kassman, 'Libya Wrap (L O)', 20 December 2003, via GlobalSecurity.Org: http://www.globalsecurity.org/wmd/library/news/libya/libya-031220-3ee73869.htm; 'Libya meets with UN

nuclear inspectors', Reuters, 20 December 2003; 'The New Gadhafi', *60 Minutes*.

11 'Rid Africa of weapons of mass destruction', *Pretoria News*, 1 March 2004, p. 2, via Independent Online: http://www.int.iol.co.za/index.php?set_id=1&click_id=68&art_id=vn20040301024056771C535508.

12 Kassman, 'Libya Wrap'.

13 Kerr, 'IAEA praises Libya for disarmament efforts'.

14 'Statement by the Prime Minister, Tony Blair', Durham, United Kingdom, 19 December 2003: http://www.number10.gov.uk/output/Page5077.asp.

15 Kerr, 'IAEA praises Libya for disarmament efforts'.

16 Dejevsky, 'Libya decided 10 years ago against developing WMD without pressure, Foreign Minister says', p. 6.

17 'President Bush: Libya Pledges to Dismantle WMD Programs', The White House, 19 December 2003: http://www.whitehouse.gov/news/releases/2003/12/20031219-9.html.

18 'The President's National Security Strategy to Combat WMD: Libya's Announcement', Fact Sheet (Washington DC: The White House, 19 December 2003), via US State Department: http://www.state.gov/p/nea/rls/27462.htm.

19 DeSutter, Hearing before the Subcommittee on International Terrorism, Nonproliferation and Human Rights, Committee on International Relations, US House of Representatives, 22 September 2004: http://wwwa.house.gov/international_relations/108/deso92204.htm.

20 Gertz, 'Libyan sincerity on arms in doubt'.

21 St John, 'Libya is Not Iraq: Preemptive Strikes, WMD and Diplomacy', *Middle East Journal*, vol. 58, no. 3, Summer 2004, p. 401.

22 Stephen D. Collins, 'Dissuading State Support of Terrorism: Strikes or Sanctions? An Analysis of Dissuasion Measures Employed Against Libya', *Studies in Conflict and Terrorism*, vol. 27, no. 1, January–February 2004, p. 13.

23 See Mark, 'CRS Issue Brief for Congress: Libya', p. 3; Ray Takeyh, 'Qadhafi and the Challenge of Militant Islam', *The Washington Quarterly*, vol. 21, no. 3, Summer 1998, p. 163; Collins, 'Dissuading State Support of Terrorism', p. 12.

24 James Wyllie, 'Libya: regime stress', *Jane's Intelligence Review*, vol. 21, no. 7, December 1995, pp. 554–5.

25 Katzman, Congressional Research Service, 'CRS Report for Congress: The Iran–Libya Sanctions Act (ILSA)', (Washington DC: The Library of Congress, 31 July 2003), p. 2.

26 Collins, 'Dissuading State Support of Terrorism', p. 11.

27 Mark, 'CRS Issue Brief for Congress: Libya', pp. 5–7.

28 *Ibid.*, pp. 3, 5–7.

29 *International Petroleum Monthly*, Energy Information Administration, US Department of Energy: http://www.eia.doe.gov/ipm/.

30 St John, 'Libyan Foreign Policy', p. 469.

31 'Report on United States Barriers to Trade And Investment 2004' (Brussels: European Commission, December 2004), p. 11: http://www.sice.oas.org/geograph/north/eureportonus.pdf.

32 At least two types of the following sanctions had to be imposed under ILSA (Section 6): (1) denial of export–import bank loans, credits or credit guarantees for US exports to the sanctioned firm; (2) denial of licences for the US export of military or militarily useful technology to the sanctioned firm; (3) denial of US bank loans exceeding US$10m in one year to the sanctioned firm; (4) if the sanctioned firm is a financial institution, a prohibition on that firm's service as a primary dealer in US government bonds and/or a prohibition on that firm's service as a repository for US government funds; (5) prohibition on US government procurement from the sanctioned firm; (6) a restriction on imports from the sanctioned firm, in accordance with the International Emergency Economic Powers Act. See

Katzman, 'CRS Report for Congress: The Iran–Libya Sanctions Act (ILSA)', pp. 2–3.

33   *Ibid.*, p. 4.

34   St John, 'Libyan Foreign Policy', p. 469.

35   Joffé, 'Libya and Europe', pp. 75–92.

36   St John, 'Libyan Foreign Policy', p. 469.

37   Ogunbadejo, 'Qaddafi's North African Design', p. 155.

38   Alison Pargeter, 'Libya: All change for no change', *The World Today*, August–September 2000, pp. 29–31.

39   See Collins, 'Dissuading State Support of Terrorism', p. 11; Takeyh, 'Qadhafi and the Challenge of Militant Islam', p. 163.

40   Viorst, 'The Colonel in His Labyrinth', pp. 71–2.

41   See Neil Ford, 'Libya Springs a Surprise', *The Middle East*, February 2004, pp. 32–5; 'Libya', *Country Analysis Briefs*, Energy Information Administration, US Department of Energy, January 2004: http://www.eia.doe.gov/emeu/cabs/libya.html; 'Beating Swords Into Oil Shares', *Economist*, 30 December 2003.

42   'Beating Swords into Oil Shares', *Economist*.

43   'Libya WMD Pledge: Result of Iraq War or 'Persistent Diplomacy'?', Issue Focus, US Department of State International Information Programes, Office of Research, 24 December 2003, via GlobalSecurity.Org: http://www.globalsecurity.org/wmd/library/news/libya/wwwh31225.htm.

44   Binyon, 'West beats path to forgive Libya its pariah status', *The Times*, 18 January 2005; 'Beating Swords into Oil Shares', *Economist*.

45   'Libya', *Country Analysis Briefs*, US Department of Energy, July 2004; Ford, 'Libya edges back into fold', *The Middle East*, October 2003, pp. 46–9.

46   Binyon, 'West beats path to forgive Libya its pariah status'; 'Libya', *Country Analysis Briefs*, US Department of Energy, January 2004.

47   Pargeter, 'Libya: All change for no change', p. 30; 'Beating Swords into Oil Shares', *Economist*. Beyond the general populous, the sanctions also undermined the capabilities and preparedness of Libya's armed forces, with the air force hit particularly hard by the aviation embargo. Collins, 'Dissuading State Support of Terrorism', p. 11.

48   Pargeter, 'Libya: All change for no change', pp. 30–31; Binyon, 'West beats path to forgive Libya its pariah status'.

49   Takeyh, 'Qadhafi and the Challenge of Militant Islam', pp. 167–8.

50   *Ibid.*

51   St John, 'Libyan Foreign Policy', pp. 473–4.

52   St John, 'Libya is Not Iraq', p. 390.

53   Sharon Squassoni, Congressional Research Service, 'CRS Report for Congress: Globalizing Cooperative Threat Reduction: A Survey of Options' (Washington DC: The Library of Congress, 15 April 2004), pp. 8–9: http://fpc.state.gov/documents/organization/32006.pdf.

54   Alterman and Morrison, 'Is it Time to Engage Libya?'

55   St John, 'Libyan Foreign Policy', p. 465.

56   See Neumann, Speech to the Middle East Institute, 30 November 1999: http://www.fas.org/news/libya/991130-libya-usia1.htm.

57   Joffé, 'Libya and Europe', p. 87.

58   St John, 'Libyan Foreign Policy', p. 476.

59   The ANO was created in 1974 when Abu Nidal broke away from the PLO after Yasser Arafat proposed establishing a national authority in the Gaza Strip and the West Bank 'as a step toward Palestinian statehood'. See 'Abu Nidal Organization', Council on Foreign Relations, http://www.cfr.org/publication/9153/#6; Kenneth Katzman, CRS Report for Congress, 'Terrorism: Near Eastern Groups and State Sponsors'.

60   Neumann, Speech to the Middle East Institute, 30 November 1999.

61   'Neumann's Senate Testimony on US Policy Toward Libya', 4 May 2000.

62   Neumann, Speech to the Middle East Institute, 30 November 1999.

63   Ford, 'Libya edges back into fold', pp. 46–9.

64   'Qadhafi's helping hand', Editorial, *Middle East International*, no. 716, 8 January 2004.

65 Joffé, 'Libya and Europe', p. 87. See also Collins, 'Dissuading State Support of Terrorism', p. 12; St John, 'Libyan Foreign Policy', pp. 465–6.

66 Collins, 'Dissuading State Support of Terrorism', p. 12.

67 Alterman and Morrison, 'Is it Time to Engage Libya?'

68 St John, 'Libyan Foreign Policy', p. 464.

69 Konstantinos Magliveras, 'Quaddafi's Libya and the African Union', *Perihelion* Articles , (Larnaca: European Rim Policy and Investment Council, March 2003): http://www.erpic.org/perihelion/articles2003/march/libya.htm.

70 Collins, 'Dissuading State Support of Terrorism', p. 14.

71 St John, 'Libyan Foreign Policy', pp. 465–8; Mark, 'CRS Issue Brief for Congress: Libya', pp. 5–7

72 Pargeter, 'Libya: All change for no change', p. 29; Mark, 'CRS Issue Brief for Congress: Libya', pp. 5–7.

73 Gadhafi kept tight control in the fields of foreign affairs, defence, justice, finance and security. Pargeter, 'Libya: All change for no change', p. 29.

74 James Badcock, 'Coming in from the Cold', *Africa Today*, February 2004, pp. 10–11.

75 'Libya', *Country Analysis Briefs*, Energy Information Administration, US Department of Energy, January 2004.

76 Ford, 'Libya edges back into fold', pp. 46–9.

77 Dejevsky, 'Libya decided 10 years ago against developing WMD without pressure, Foreign Minister says', p. 6.

78 St John, 'Libyan Foreign Policy', p. 464. A notable example of Libya seeking to engage the United States at this time involved Gary Hart, the former Colorado Senator and Democratic presidential candidate, who was contacted by a Libyan operative during a business trip to Greece in February 1992. Hart was asked to communicate a message to the Bush administration from Gadhafi, but was told by a State Department official that there would be 'no discussions with the Libyans until they turn over the Pan Am bombers'. As St John notes, Hart was also told that the Libyans had made other similar approaches but none had been treated seriously. Despite Washington's response Hart travelled to Libya in March 1992 where he met Jalloud, Gadhafi's long-time friend and fellow revolutionary, and Musa Kusa, the Head of External Intelligence, who served as his permanent escort. During the visit Hart told his hosts that any discussion of exchanging the Lockerbie suspects for negotiations to suspend sanctions and normalise relations would also need to encompass a verifiable end to terrorist activities and the giving up of WMD. Jalloud reportedly replied saying that, 'Everything will be on the table' (See St John, 'Libya is Not Iraq', pp. 388–9). In January 1992, Mohammed Bukhres, a Libyan-American with close ties to Gadhafi's sons, arranged for William Rogers, undersecretary of state for economic affairs during the Ford administration, to meet with Gadhafi in Libya. Rogers reportedly told the Libyan leader that he would need to turn over the Lockerbie suspects, demonstrate his renunciation of terrorism, stop interfering in other African countries and 'offer full inspection of chemical, biological and nuclear weapons facilities' (See Barbara Slavin, 'Libya's rehabilitation in the works since early '90s'.

79 Frantz and Meyer, 'The Deal to Disarm Kadafi', *Los Angeles Times*, 13 March 2005.

80 Joffé, 'Libya: Who Blinked and Why', *Current History*, vol. 103, no. 673, May 2004, p. 221.

81 St John, 'Libyan Foreign Policy', p. 470.

82 Joffé, 'Libya and Europe', p. 87.

83 Viorst, 'The Colonel in His Labyrinth', p. 73.

84 St John, 'Libya is Not Iraq', p. 398.

85 Michele Dunne, 'Libya: Security is Not Enough', *Policy Brief 32* (Washington DC: Carnegie Endowment for International Peace, October 2004) pp. 1–7: http://www.carnegieendowment.org/publications/index.cfm?fa=view&id=15921&prog=zgp&proj=zdrl.

86 Fidler, Huband and Roula Khalaf, 'Return to the fold: how Gaddaffi was persuaded to give up his nuclear goals', *Financial Times*, 27 July 2004, p. 17.

87 Martin S. Indyk, 'The Iraq War did not Force Gadaffi's Hand', *Financial Times*, 9 March 2004; Flynt L. Leverett, 'Why Libya Gave Up on the Bomb', *New York Times*, 23 January 2004; St John, 'Libya is Not Iraq', pp. 390–92; Kerr, 'IAEA praises Libya for disarmament efforts'; Slavin, 'Libya's rehabilitation in the works since early '90s'.

88 Indyk, 'The Iraq War did not force Gaddafi's Hand'; See also Joffé, 'Why Gaddafi gave up WMD', BBC News Online, 21 December 2003: http://news.bbc.co.uk/1/hi/world/africa/3338713.stm.

89 Intelligence on Libya's involvement with the A.Q. Khan network began to emerge in 2000. 'Report to the President of the United States', The Commission on the Intelligence Capabilities of the US Regarding WMD, p. 257.

90 Indyk, 'The Iraq War did not Force Gadaffi's Hand'; Leverett, 'Why Libya Gave Up on the Bomb'; St John, 'Libya is Not Iraq', pp. 390–92; Kerr, 'IAEA praises Libya for disarmament efforts'.; Slavin, 'Libya's rehabilitation in the works since early '90s'.

91 Slavin, 'Libya's rehabilitation in the works since early '90s'.

92 St John, 'Libyan Foreign Policy', pp. 472–3.

93 Slavin, 'Libya's rehabilitation in the works since early '90s'.

94 St John, 'Libyan Foreign Policy', pp. 473–4.

95 Kerr, 'IAEA praises Libya for disarmament efforts'.

96 Leverett, 'Why Libya Gave Up on the Bomb'.

97 *Ibid.*

98 Mark, 'CRS Issue Brief for Congress: Libya', p. 4. According to an article published in the *Observer* on 7 October 2001, Musa Kusa arrived in London for talks with members of the British Secret Intelligence Service and the CIA: Nick Pelham, 'Libyan linked to Lockerbie welcome in UK War on Terrorism', *Observer*, 7 October 2001.

99 Statement by Mr Abdulrahman M. Shalgham, secretary of the General People's Committee for Foreign Liaison and International Cooperation at the Conference on Facilitating the Entry into Force of the Comprehensive Test Ban Treaty, New York, 13 November 2001.

100 St John, 'Libya is Not Iraq', p. 394.

101 Squassoni and Andrew Feickert, Congressional Research Service, 'CRS Report for Congress: Disarming Libya: Weapons of Mass Destruction' (Washington DC: The Library of Congress, 22 April 2004), p. 3: http://fpc.state.gov/documents/organization/32007.pdf.

102 Joffé, 'Libya: Who Blinked and Why', p. 223.

103 *Ibid.*; Joffé, 'Fear or Calculation?', *Middle East International*, 9 January 2004, pp. 9–10.

104 Michael Smith, 'Blair may take credit, but it was all down to an MI6 spy in a Bedouin tent', *Daily Telegraph*, 22 December 2003, p. 4.

105 Dejevsky, 'Libya decided 10 years ago against developing WMD without pressure, Foreign Minister says', p. 6.

106 Joffé, 'Fear or Calculation?', pp. 9–10;'Libya: Who Blinked and Why', p. 223.

107 St John, 'Libya is Not Iraq', p. 398.

108 Fidler, Huband and Khalaf, 'Return to the fold: how Gaddaffi was persuaded to give up his nuclear goals'.

109 Michael Evans, 'Libya knew game was up before Iraq war', *The Times*, 13 March 2004, p. 8; Frantz and Meyer, 'The Deal to Disarm Kadafi'; Gertz, 'Libyan sincerity on arms in doubt'.

110 'Saif Qadhafi', GlobalSecurity.Org: http://www.globalsecurity.org/military/world/libya/saif-qadhafi.htm; Golnaz Esfandiari, 'Libya: Analysts Say Decision On WMD Inspired By Economics, Worries About Succession', Radio Free Europe, 22 December 2003; Brian Whitaker, 'US tests the air in reformed Libya', *Guardian*, 26 January 2004, p. 13.

111 Seif al-Islam Qadhafi, 'Libyan–American Relations', *Middle East Policy*, vol. 10, no. 1, Spring 2003, pp. 43–44..

112 Evans, 'Libya knew game was up before Iraq war', p. 8.

113 President George W. Bush, 'State of the Union Address', 20 January 2004: http://www.whitehouse.gov/news/releases/2004/01/20040120-7.html.

114 Robin Gedye, 'UN should fight for rights, says Berlusconi', *Daily Telegraph*, 4 September 2003; James Kirchich, 'Democratic critics are delusional about implications of the Bush Doctrine', *Yale Daily News*, 16 January 2004.

115 Evans, 'Libya knew game was up before Iraq war', p. 8.

116 *Ibid.*

117 Leverett, 'Why Libya Gave Up on the Bomb'.

118 Michael Hirsh, 'Bolton's British Problem: Fresh complaints of bullying dog an embattled nominee', *Newsweek*, 2 May 2005.

119 Frantz and Meyer, 'The Deal to Disarm Kadafi'; Gertz, 'Libyan sincerity on arms in doubt'.

120 'US will not oppose ending of UN sanctions on Libya', Statement by the Press Secretary, 15 August 2003, The White House: http://www.globalsecurity. org/security/library/news/2003/08/sec-030815-usia04.htm.

121 'The UN Security Council has voted 13–0 to lift sanctions against Libya that were imposed in response to the 1988 bombing of PanAm Flight 103 over Lockerbie, Scotland', CNN, 12 September 2003.

122 The White House, 'US will not oppose ending of UN sanctions on Libya'; CNN, 'The UN Security Council has voted 13–0 to lift sanctions against Libya that were imposed in response to the 1988 bombing of PanAm Flight 103 over Lockerbie, Scotland'.

123 St John, 'Libya is Not Iraq', pp. 396–7.

124 See interview on *This Week with George Stephanopoulos*, ABC News (US), 4 August 2003; 'Libya ready for inspections', News 24 (South Africa), 4 August 2003.

125 Evans, 'Libya knew game was up before Iraq war', p. 8.

126 'Report to the President of the United States', The Commission on the Intelligence Capabilities of the US Regarding WMD, p. 257.

127 'Review of Intelligence on Weapons of Mass Destruction', Report of a Committee of Privy Counsellors, House of Commons (London: The Stationery Office, 14 July 2004), p. 18.

128 According to a different school of thought, however, the Libyans themselves provided information on the *BBC China* as a gesture to demonstrate the country's commitment to giving up WMD. For example, a report in the *Guardian* attributed this line of argument to close followers of nuclear proliferation issues who are convinced that the *BBC China* was interdicted because of information provided by the Libyans. Traynor, 'Libya's black market deals shock nuclear inspectors', *Guardian*, 17 January 2004.

129 Frantz and Meyer, 'The Deal to Disarm Kadafi'.

130 'Report to the President of the United States', The Commission on the Intelligence Capabilities of the US Regarding WMD, p.252.

131 Frantz and Meyer, 'The Deal to Disarm Kadafi'; DeSutter, 'US Government's Assistance to Libya in the Elimination of its Weapons of Mass Destruction (WMD)', Testimony before the Senate Foreign Relations Committee, 26 February 2004: http://www.globalsecurity.org/wmd/library/congress/2004_h/DeSutterTestimony040226.pdf; Mahley, 'Dismantling Libyan Weapons'; DeSutter, Testimony before the Senate Foreign Relations Committee, 26 February 2004; Frantz and Meyer, 'The Deal to Disarm Kadafi'.

132 *Ibid.*

133 *Ibid.*

134 'Report to the President of the United States', The Commission on the Intelligence Capabilities of the US Regarding WMD, p. 254.

[135] Conoco-Phillips and Marathon each have 16.3% of the oil concessions. Amerada Hess has 8.2% while the remaining 59.2% is held by Libya's NOC. Greg Flakus, 'US Oil Companies Re-Enter Libya', Voice of America News, 2 January 2006.

[136] Viorst, 'The Colonel in His Labyrinth', p. 72.

[137] Joffé, 'Libya: Who Blinked and Why', p. 224.

[138] 'Libya', Country Analysis Briefs, Energy Information Administration, US Department of Energy, January 2004.

Chapter Four

[1] Mahley, 'Dismantling Libyan Weapons', p. 4.

[2] DeSutter, Hearing before the Subcommittee on International Terrorism, Nonproliferation and Human Rights, 22 September 2004.

[3] The British and American governments helped Libya to get involved with the OPCW because it was not a member. This was obviously not the case with the IAEA.

[4] 'IAEA Director General to Visit Libya', IAEA Press Release 2003/14, 22 December 2003: http://www.iaea.org/NewsCenter/PressReleases/2003/prn200314.html.

[5] 'IAEA Verification of Libya's Nuclear Programme: Board Adopts Resolution, Libya Signs Additional Protocol', IAEA Staff Report, 10 March 2004: http://www.iaea.org/NewsCenter/News/2004/libya_ap1003.html.

[6] 'Libya ratifies the CTBT', Comprehensive Test Ban Treaty Organisation Press Release, 14 January 2004: http://www.ctbto.org/press_centre/press_release.dhtml?item=217; 'Libya signs accord for enhanced inspections by UN nuclear watchdog agency', UN News Service, 10 March 2004: http://www.un.org/apps/news/story.asp?NewsID=10026&Cr=libya&Cr1=.

[7] DeSutter, Testimony before the Senate Foreign Relations Committee, 26 February 2004.

[8] See Patrick E. Tyler, 'Libya's Atom Bid in Early Phases', New York Times, 30 December, 2003; Louis Charbonneau, 'Libya never got nuclear plans off ground-Diplomats', Reuters, 15 January 2004; 'Libya meets with UN nuclear inspec-tors', Reuters, 20 December 2003; 'Nuke Teams Set To Disarm Libya', CBS News, 20 January 2004.

[9] Jack Boureston and Yana Feldman, 'Verifying Libya's Nuclear Disarmament', Verification Yearbook 2004 (London: VERTIC 2003), pp. 90–92: http://www.vertic.org/assets/YB04/Boureston-Feldman%209.pdf.

[10] 'ElBaradei: Libya helping with nuclear black market "puzzle"', USA Today, 24 February 2004.

[11] DeSutter, Testimony before the Senate Foreign Relations Committee, 26 February 2004.

[12] Boureston and Feldman, 'Verifying Libya's Nuclear Disarmament', pp. 90–92.

[13] DeSutter, Hearing before the Subcommittee on International Terrorism, Nonproliferation and Human Rights, 22 September 2004.

[14] 'Madmen, Rogues & Nukes', MSNBC News, 11 October 2004.

[15] DeSutter, Hearing before the Subcommittee on International Terrorism, Nonproliferation and Human Rights, 22 September 2004; DeSutter, 'Weapons of Mass Destruction, Terrorism, Human Rights and the Future of US–Libyan Relations', Testimony before the House International Relations Committee, 10 March 2004, http://www.state.gov/t/vc/rls/rm/2004/30347.htm; Director General, IAEA, Implementation of the NPT Safeguards Agreement, 28 May 2004, pp. 4–5.

[16] DeSutter, Testimony before the Senate Foreign Relations Committee, 26 February 2004.

[17] DeSutter, Hearing before the Subcommittee on International Terrorism,

Nonproliferation and Human Rights, 22 September 2004.

[18] Dunne, 'Libya: Security is Not Enough', pp. 1–7.

[19] Squassoni and Feickert, 'CRS Report for Congress: Disarming Libya', p. 3.

[20] Joffé, 'Libya: Who Blinked and Why', p. 225.

[21] DeSutter, Hearing before the Subcommittee on International Terrorism, Nonproliferation and Human Rights, 22 September 2004.

[22] 'Removal of High-Enriched Uranium in Libyan Arab Jamahiriya', IAEA Staff Report, 8 March 2004: http://www.iaea. org/NewsCenter/News/2004/libya_ uranium0803.html; DeSutter, Testimony before the Senate Foreign Relations Committee, 26 February 2004; 'Libya Sends Tajura HEU to Russia, Prepares to Convert Reactor to LEU', *NuclearFuel*, vol. 29, no. 6, 15 March 2004, p. 4.

[23] 'US Eases Economic Embargo Against Libya', The White House, Office of the Press Secretary, 23 April 2004: http:// www.whitehouse.gov/news/releases/200 4/04/20040423-9.html.

[24] DeSutter, Hearing before the Subcommittee on International Terrorism, Nonproliferation and Human Rights, 22 September 2004.

[25] Salah Sarrar, 'US Resumes Diplomatic Ties With Libya', *Reuters*, 28 June 2004.

[26] 'Blair Visits Libya, Continuing a Thaw', *Associated Press*, 25 March 2004.

[27] 'Libyan Leader Embraces West', BBC News Online, 27 April 2004 .

[28] DeSutter, Hearing before the Subcommittee on International Terrorism, Nonproliferation and Human Rights, 22 September 2004.

[29] 'Memorandum for the Secretary of State', Presidential Determination No. 2004-44, 10 September 2004, The White House: http://www.whitehouse.gov.edgesuite. net/news/releases/2004/09/20040910-12.html.

[30] Kerr, 'Libya Pledges Military Trade Curbs, but Details Are Fuzzy', *Arms Control Today*, June 2004: http://www.armscontrol.org/act/2004_06/Libya.asp.

[31] Bolton, 'Libya Ending Military Trade with States of Serious Weapons of Mass Destruction Proliferation Concern', Daily Press Briefing, 13 May 2004: http://www. state.gov/p/nea/rls/rm/32491.htm; Kerr, 'Libya Pledges Military Trade Curbs, but Details Are Fuzzy'.

[32] 'State Department Highlights Positive Developments in Libya', 21 September 2004, Office of the Spokesman, US State Department: http://usinfo.state.gov/xar-chives/display.html?p=washfile-english& y=2004&m=September&x=2004092119003 3ndyblehs0.3046381.

[33] Judy Aita, 'Powell Meets with Libyan Foreign Minister', *Washington File*, US State Department, 24 September 2004.

[34] Binyon, 'West beats path to forgive Libya its pariah status'; Michael Knipe, 'Libya set for European embrace', *The Times*, 18 January 2005; 'Gaddafi's son being groomed to take over', *The Straits Times* (Singapore), 15 October 2004; Ahto Lobjakas, 'EU: Arms Embargo on Libya Lifted, But Decision On China Delayed', Radio Free Europe/Radio Liberty, 12 October 2004.

[35] DeSutter, Hearing before the Subcommittee on International Terrorism, Nonproliferation and Human Rights, 22 September 2004.

[36] Outstanding issues in the chemical arena included the destruction of chemical agents and precursors. Libya was given five years to convert its *Scud*-B ballistic missiles to fall within the parameters of the MTCR (300km range, 500kg payload).

[37] 'Russia Delivers Low-Enriched Uranium To Libya', Radio Free Europe/Radio Liberty, 23 December 2005..

[38] Kerr, 'IAEA: Questions Remain About Libya'.

[39] 'Report: Libya, Egypt Swapped Nukes', *United Press International*, 31 March 2004.

[40] Mahley, 'Dismantling Libyan Weapons', p. 7. See also Khalaf and Fidler, 'Safe jobs sought for Libya's weapons scientists', *Financial Times*, 30 April 2004, p. 8.

[41] 'President Announces New Measures to Counter the Threat of WMD', Remarks by

President G. W. Bush, National Defense University, 11 February 2004: http://www.whitehouse.gov/news/releases/2004/02/20040211-4.html.

42 Squassoni and Feickert, 'CRS Report for Congress: Disarming Libya', p. 6.

43 'Countering the Proliferation of Weapons of Mass Destruction', Written Ministerial Statement by Straw, UK Foreign and Commonwealth Office, 25 February 2004: http://www.fco.gov.uk/servlet/Front?pagename=OpenMarket/Xcelerate/ShowPage&c=Page&cid=1007029391629&a=KArticle&aid=1077043155337.

44 Bolton, 'Lessons from Libya and North Korea's Strategic Choice', Address at Yonsei University, Seoul, South Korea, 21 July 2004: http://www.globalsecurity.org/wmd/library/news/dprk/2004/07/dprk-040721-34538pf.htm.

45 Richard Stone, 'Agencies Plan Exchange With Libya's Former Weaponeers', pp. 185–6.

Conclusion

1 He made these remarks during his visit to the European Union in 2004. Michael Thurnston, 'Kadhafi Urges World to Follow his Lead, Give Up Weapons of Mass Destruction', *Agence France-Presse*, 27 April 2004.

RECENT **ADELPHI PAPERS** INCLUDE:

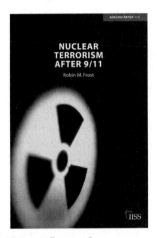

ADELPHI PAPER 378
Nuclear Terrorism After 9/11
Robin M. Frost
ISBN 0-415-39992-0

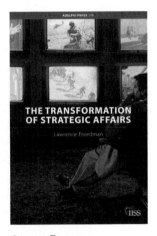

ADELPHI PAPER 379
The Transformation of Strategic Affairs
Lawrence Freedman
ISBN 0-415-40724-9